SPECTRUM

Grade 1

Published by Spectrum®
an imprint of Carson-Dellosa Publishing
Greensboro, NC

Spectrum®
An imprint of Carson-Dellosa Publishing LLC
P.O. Box 35665
Greensboro, NC 27425 USA

© 2015 Carson-Dellosa Publishing LLC. Except as permitted under the United States Copyright Act, no part of this publication may be reproduced, stored, or distributed in any form or by any means (mechanically, electronically, recording, etc.) without the prior written consent of Carson-Dellosa Publishing LLC. Spectrum® is an imprint of Carson-Dellosa Publishing LLC.

Printed in the USA • All rights reserved.   ISBN 978-1-4838-1625-8

02-032167784

Table of Contents Grade 1

Math
Chapter 1: Addition and Subtraction Facts Through 10 6
Chapter 2: Place Value 29
Chapter 3: Addition and Subtraction Facts Through 20 40
Chapter 4: Addition and Subtraction Facts Through 100 57
Chapter 5: Measurement 62
Chapter 6: Geometry 73

Language Arts
Chapter 1: Grammar
Parts of Speech 82
Sentences 93
Chapter 2: Mechanics
Capitalization 103
Punctuation 113
Chapter 3: Usage 125
Chapter 4: Writer's Guide 153

Reading
Little Duck 160
Carolyn Dreams of a Pet 208
Nonfiction 244

Answer Key 276

Note: Due to content, the nonfiction passages on pages 244-269 have more advanced vocabulary. These passages may need to be read with a teacher or parent guide depending on the child's reading level.

Lesson 1.18 Problem Solving

SHOW YOUR WORK

Solve each problem.

There are 8 🛒.
There are 2 🛒.
What is the sum? __10__

$$\begin{array}{r} 8 \\ +2 \\ \hline 10 \end{array}$$

There are 6 🦛.
3 more 🦛 come.
What is 6 plus 3? _____

I have 4 🖊.
I buy 4 more 🖊.
How many do I have now? _____

Ivan has 2 🦖.
Helen has 5 🦖.
What is 2 + 5? _____

There are 7 🐦.
3 more 🐦 come.
How many in all? _____

Spectrum Grade 1
23

Lesson 1.19 Adding with Money

I penny
1¢

I nickel
5¢

I dime
10¢

Add and write how much money.

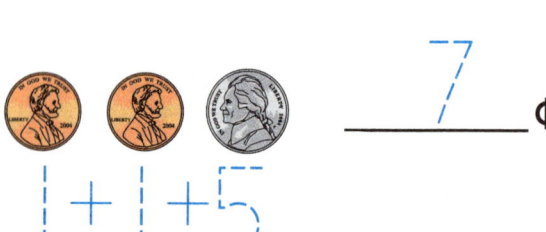 7 ¢

 _____ ¢

 _____ ¢

 _____ ¢

 _____ ¢

 _____ ¢

 _____ ¢

Spectrum Grade 1

NAME _____

Lesson 1.20 Problem Solving

SHOW YOUR WORK

Solve each problem.

John has 10¢.
He buys 🚗 for 3¢.
How much money does he have left? ___7___ ¢

$$\begin{array}{r} 10 \\ -3 \\ \hline 7 \end{array}$$

Ines buys 🧸 for 6¢.
She buys 🐛 for 4¢.
How much money did she spend? _____ ¢

Jordan has 3¢.
He finds 5¢.
How much money does he have? _____ ¢

Elaine has 9¢.
She gives 4¢ to Maxine.
How much money does Elaine have left? _____ ¢

Victor has 7¢.
He buys ✏️ for 6¢.
How much money does he have left? _____ ¢

Lin buys 🍑 for 5¢.
Barb buys 🍎 for 4¢.
How much money did they spend? _____ ¢

Spectrum Grade 1
25

Lesson 1.21 More- and Less-Than Facts through 10

SHOW YOUR WORK

Add to find more than. Subtract to find less than.

How many is 2 more than 7 ? __9__ $2 + 7 = 9$

What is 1 more than 8 ? _____

There are 2 less than 10 .
How many  are there? _____

What is 1 less than 9 ? _____

There is 1 more than 7 .
How many are there? _____

What is 2 less than 8 ? _____

How many is 1 less than 10 ? _____

How many is 1 more than 9 ? _____

There is 1 less than 8 .
How many are there? _____

Spectrum Grade 1

Lesson 1.22 Using Addition for Subtraction

Think addition for subtraction. Solve each problem.

8 − 4 = __4__   4 + ____ = 8

10 − 3 = ____   3 + ____ = 10

7 − 2 = ____   2 + ____ = 7

10 − 4 = ____   4 + ____ = 10

5 − 1 = ____   1 + ____ = 5

8 − 2 = ____   2 + ____ = 8

9 − 7 = ____   7 + ____ = 9

7 − 6 = ____   6 + ____ = 7

8 − 5 = ____   5 + ____ = 8

Lesson 1.23 Doubles and Near-Doubles

NAME _____

Add to find the sum.

   2
   +2
   4

3 + 3 = __6__ + 1 = __7__

1 + 1 = _____ + 1 = _____

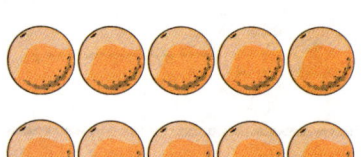   5
   +5

   3
   +3

4 + 4 = _____ + 1 = _____

   4
   +4

   1
   +1

2 + 2 = _____ + 1 = _____

3 + 3 = _____ + 1 = _____

Spectrum Grade 1

Chapter 2

Lesson 2.1 Counting and Writing 10 through 14

NAME _____

Complete.

   __1__ ten __0__ ones = __10__

   ____ ten ____ one = _____

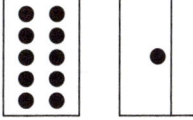   ____ ten ____ ones = _____

   ____ ten ____ ones = _____

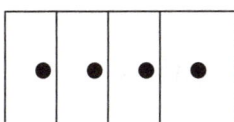   ____ ten ____ ones = _____

Spectrum Grade 1

Lesson 2.2 Counting and Writing 15 through 19

Complete.

 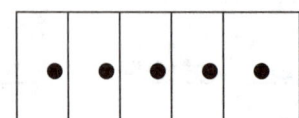 $\underline{1}$ ten $\underline{5}$ ones = $\underline{15}$

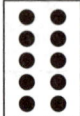 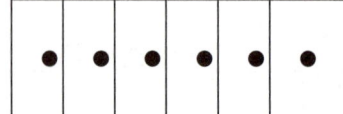   ___ ten ___ ones = _____

 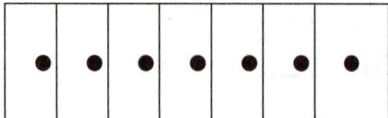   ___ ten ___ ones = _____

 ___ ten ___ ones = _____

 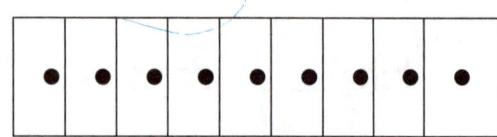   ___ ten ___ ones = _____

Lesson 2.3 Counting and Writing 20 through 24

Complete.

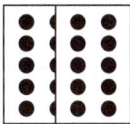   _2_ tens _0_ ones = _20_

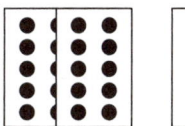    _2_ tens _1_ one = _21_

   ___ tens ___ ones = _____

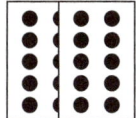   ___ tens ___ ones = _____

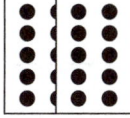   ___ tens ___ ones = _____

Lesson 2.4 Counting and Writing 25 through 29

NAME _____

Complete.

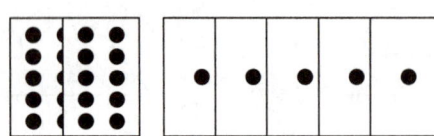   _2_ tens _5_ ones = _25_

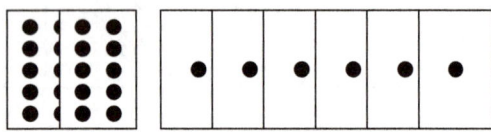   ___ tens ___ ones = _____

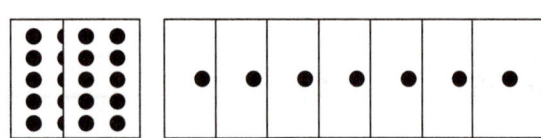   ___ tens ___ ones = _____

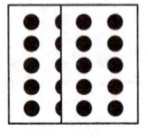 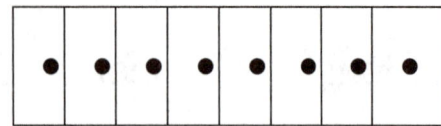   ___ tens ___ ones = _____

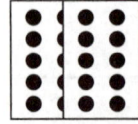 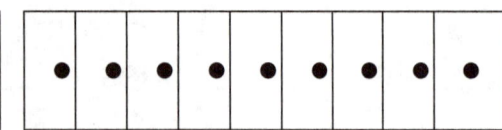 ___ tens ___ ones = _____

Spectrum Grade 1

Lesson 2.5 Counting and Writing 30 through 49

Complete.

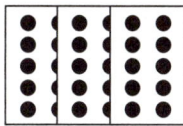 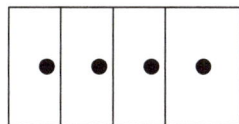 3 tens 4 ones = 34

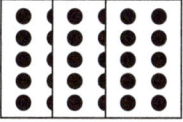 ___ tens ___ ones = ___

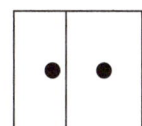 ___ tens ___ ones = ___

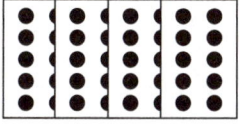 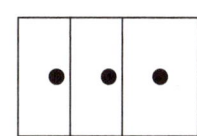 ___ tens ___ ones = ___

4 tens 4 ones = 44

3 tens 9 ones = ___

3 tens 6 ones = ___

4 tens 5 ones = ___

4 tens 1 one = ___

3 tens 7 ones = ___

3 tens 8 ones = ___

4 tens 0 ones = ___

4 tens 6 ones = ___

3 tens 3 ones = ___

Spectrum Grade 1

Lesson 2.6 Counting and Writing 50 through 69

Complete.

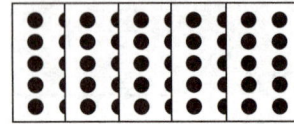 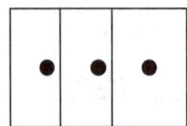   5 tens 1 ones = 51

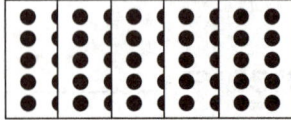 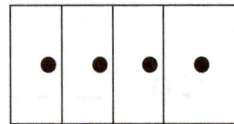   ___ tens ___ ones = _____

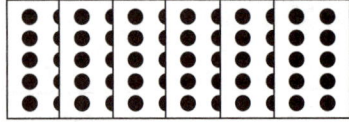 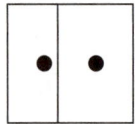   ___ tens ___ ones = _____

___ tens ___ ones = _____

6 tens 0 ones = _____   6 tens 9 ones = _____

5 tens 2 ones = _____   6 tens 4 ones = _____

6 tens 7 ones = _____   5 tens 5 ones = _____

5 tens 3 ones = _____   6 tens 6 ones = _____

5 tens 8 ones = _____   5 tens 7 ones = _____

Spectrum Grade 1

Lesson 2.7 Counting and Writing 70 through 99

Complete.

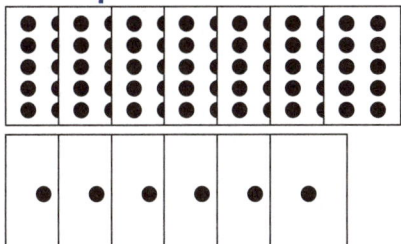

7 tens 6 ones = 76

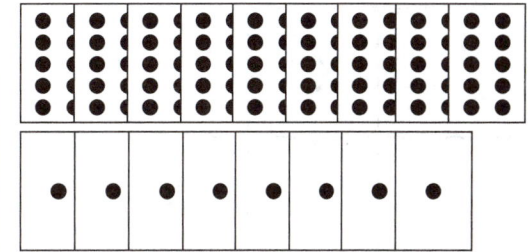

9 tens 8 ones = 98

8 tens 3 ones = 83

8 tens 0 ones = _____

7 tens 1 one = _____

7 tens 5 ones = _____

8 tens 7 ones = _____

9 tens 9 ones = _____

9 tens 4 ones = _____

9 tens 1 one = _____

9 tens 2 ones = _____

8 tens 6 ones = _____

7 tens 9 ones = _____

7 tens 0 ones = _____

8 tens 8 ones = _____

8 tens 2 ones = _____

Lesson 2.8 Counting to 120

Count forward. Write the missing numbers.

1		3				7			10
11			14		16		18		
	22			25			28		30
	32			35		37			40
	43		45					49	
51				55		57			60
61			64		66		68		
	73						78		
81				85					90
		94		96		98			
		103							
	112			115		117		119	

Lesson 2.9 Counting Forward and Backward to 120

Count forward. Write the missing numbers.

36, 37, _38_, 39, _40_, 41, 42, _43_, 44, 45, _46_

92, 93, ___, 95, 96, ___, 98, 99, ___, ___, 102, 103

___, 67, 68, ___, 70, 71, ___, 73, 74, 75, ___, 77

100, 101, ___, 103, 104, ___, 106, ___, 108, 109, ___, 111

___, 10, 15, ___, 25, 30, 35, ___, 45, 50, 55, ___

___, 20, 30, ___, 50, ___, 70, 80, ___, ___, ___, ___

Count backward. Write the missing numbers.

79, ___, 77, 76, ___, 74, 73, 72, ___, 70, 69, ___

84, ___, 82, 81, ___, 79, 78, 77, ___, ___, 74, 73

24, 22, ___, 18, 16, ___, 12, ___, 8, 6, ___, 2

120, ___, 110, 105, ___, 95, 90, ___, ___, 75, 70, 65

75, 70, ___, 60, 55, ___, 45, 40, 35, ___, 25, ___

___, ___, 90, ___, 70, 60, ___, ___, 30, ___

Spectrum Grade 1
37

Lesson 2.10 Comparing Numbers

Compare 2-digit numbers.

53 > 36   Compare tens. 5 is greater than 3. 53 is greater than 36.

73 < 76   If tens are the same, compare ones. 3 is less than 6. 73 is less than 76.

Compare 2-digit numbers. Use > (greater than), < (less than), or = (equal to).

16 __ 22		78 __ 38		86 __ 88	
37 __ 18		45 __ 45		15 __ 26	
51 __ 56		73 __ 99		92 __ 92	
70 __ 70		24 __ 25		19 __ 11	
35 __ 74		40 __ 30		48 __ 89	
81 __ 43		13 __ 13		36 __ 34	
12 __ 20		33 __ 42		63 __ 63	
62 __ 41		21 __ 17		71 __ 61	

Spectrum Grade 1
38

Lesson 2.10 Comparing Numbers

Compare 2-digit numbers. Use > (greater than), < (less than), or = (equal to).

77 < 87	97 < 98	6 < 49
90 > 80	4 < 27	69 > 58
79 > 5	46 < 75	1 < 10
53 > 32	94 > 82	50 < 93
64 = 64	67 > 29	95 > 3
84 < 96	60 > 39	15 > 11
23 > 9	55 < 72	63 = 63
57 < 85	2 < 68	59 < 83
52 > 31	91 > 8	47 > 37
47 = 47	66 < 83	50 = 50
28 > 7	14 < 59	21 < 31
44 < 54	76 > 65	35 > 23

Spectrum Grade 1

Chapter 3
NAME _____

Lesson 3.1 Adding to 11

Add.

   7
      +4
      ---
      1 1

   8
      +3

   6
      +5

   9
      +2

   4
      +7

   3
      +8

   5
      +6

   2
      +9
      ---

  5   9   4   2   7   8
 +6   +3   +7   +9   +3   +3
 ---   ---   ---   ---   ---   ---

Spectrum Grade 1

Lesson 3.2 Subtracting from 11

Subtract.

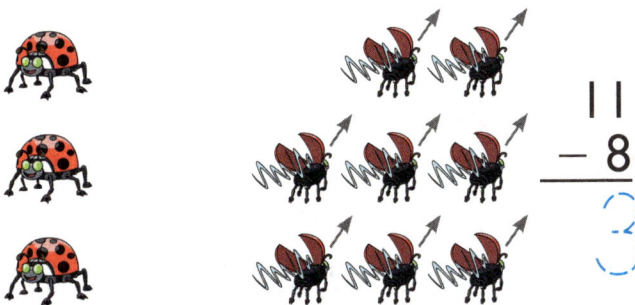 
$\begin{array}{r}11\\-8\\\hline 3\end{array}$

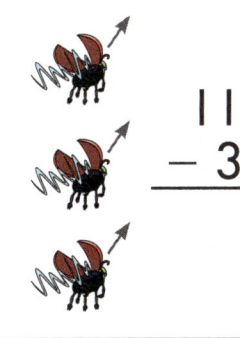
$\begin{array}{r}11\\-3\\\hline\end{array}$

 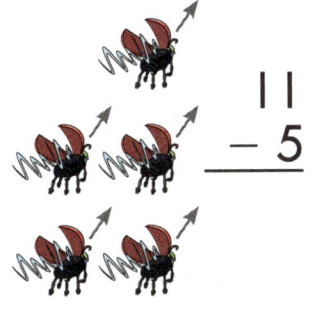
$\begin{array}{r}11\\-5\\\hline\end{array}$

 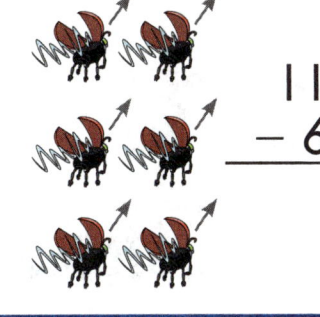
$\begin{array}{r}11\\-6\\\hline\end{array}$

 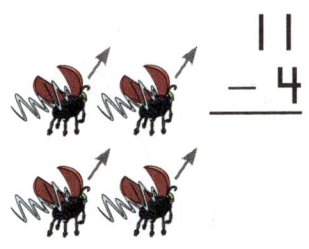
$\begin{array}{r}11\\-4\\\hline\end{array}$

 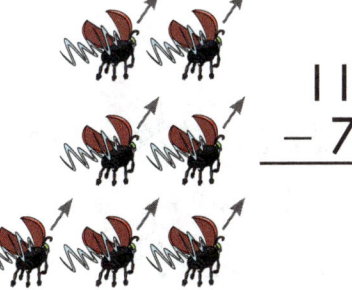
$\begin{array}{r}11\\-7\\\hline\end{array}$

$\begin{array}{r}11\\-2\\\hline\end{array}$

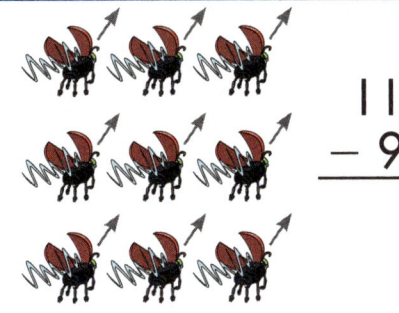
$\begin{array}{r}11\\-9\\\hline\end{array}$

$\begin{array}{r}11\\-3\\\hline\end{array}$ $\begin{array}{r}11\\-6\\\hline\end{array}$ $\begin{array}{r}11\\-9\\\hline\end{array}$ $\begin{array}{r}11\\-8\\\hline\end{array}$ $\begin{array}{r}11\\-4\\\hline\end{array}$ $\begin{array}{r}11\\-0\\\hline\end{array}$

Spectrum Grade 1

Lesson 3.3 Adding to 12

Add.

 9
+3

12

 3
+9

 4
+8

 5
+7

 7
+5

 6
+6

5	8	9	6	4	7
+8	+4	+3	+6	+9	+5

5 + 6 = _____ 8 + 4 = _____ 6 + 6 = _____

9 + 3 = _____ 7 + 5 = _____ 3 + 9 = _____

Spectrum Grade 1

Lesson 3.4 Subtracting from 12

Subtract.

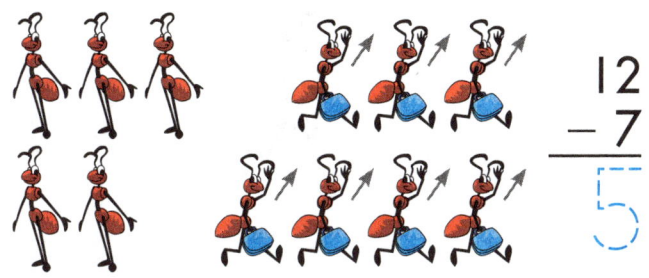
$$\begin{array}{r}12\\-\ 7\\\hline 5\end{array}$$

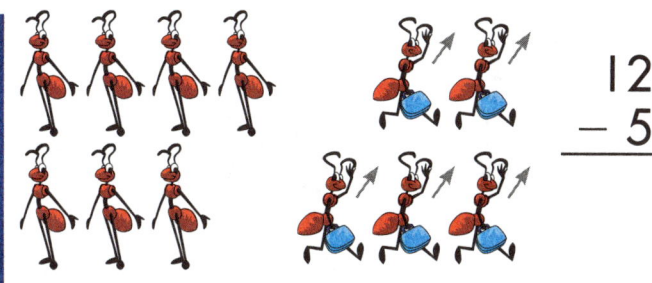
$$\begin{array}{r}12\\-\ 5\\\hline\end{array}$$

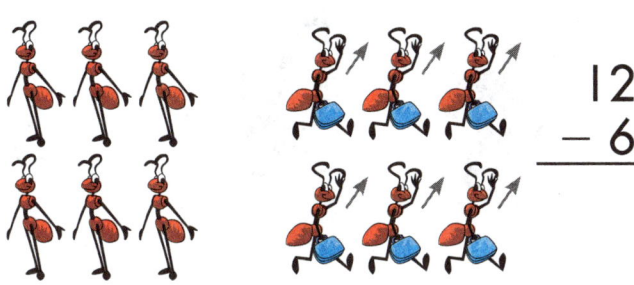
$$\begin{array}{r}12\\-\ 6\\\hline\end{array}$$

$$\begin{array}{r}12\\-\ 8\\\hline\end{array}$$

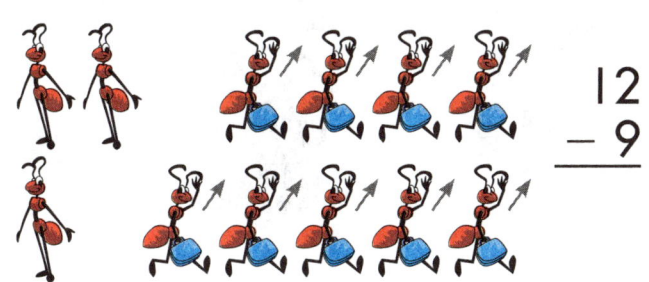
$$\begin{array}{r}12\\-\ 9\\\hline\end{array}$$

$$\begin{array}{r}12\\-\ 3\\\hline\end{array}$$

$$\begin{array}{r}12\\-\ 4\\\hline\end{array}\qquad\begin{array}{r}12\\-\ 3\\\hline\end{array}\qquad\begin{array}{r}12\\-\ 8\\\hline\end{array}\qquad\begin{array}{r}12\\-\ 7\\\hline\end{array}\qquad\begin{array}{r}12\\-\ 6\\\hline\end{array}\qquad\begin{array}{r}12\\-\ 5\\\hline\end{array}$$

12 − 9 = _____   12 − 8 = _____   12 − 6 = _____

12 − 7 = _____   12 − 3 = _____   12 − 4 = _____

Lesson 3.5 Adding to 13

Add.

  $\begin{array}{r}6\\+7\\\hline 13\end{array}$   $\begin{array}{r}7\\+6\\\hline\end{array}$

  $\begin{array}{r}4\\+9\\\hline\end{array}$   $\begin{array}{r}9\\+4\\\hline\end{array}$

  $\begin{array}{r}8\\+5\\\hline\end{array}$   $\begin{array}{r}5\\+8\\\hline\end{array}$

$\begin{array}{r}7\\+6\\\hline\end{array}$ $\begin{array}{r}5\\+8\\\hline\end{array}$ $\begin{array}{r}9\\+4\\\hline\end{array}$ $\begin{array}{r}6\\+6\\\hline\end{array}$ $\begin{array}{r}4\\+9\\\hline\end{array}$ $\begin{array}{r}8\\+5\\\hline\end{array}$

5 + 8 = _____   4 + 9 = _____   7 + 5 = _____

9 + 4 = _____   8 + 3 = _____   6 + 7 = _____

Spectrum Grade 1

Lesson 3.6 Subtracting from 13

Subtract.

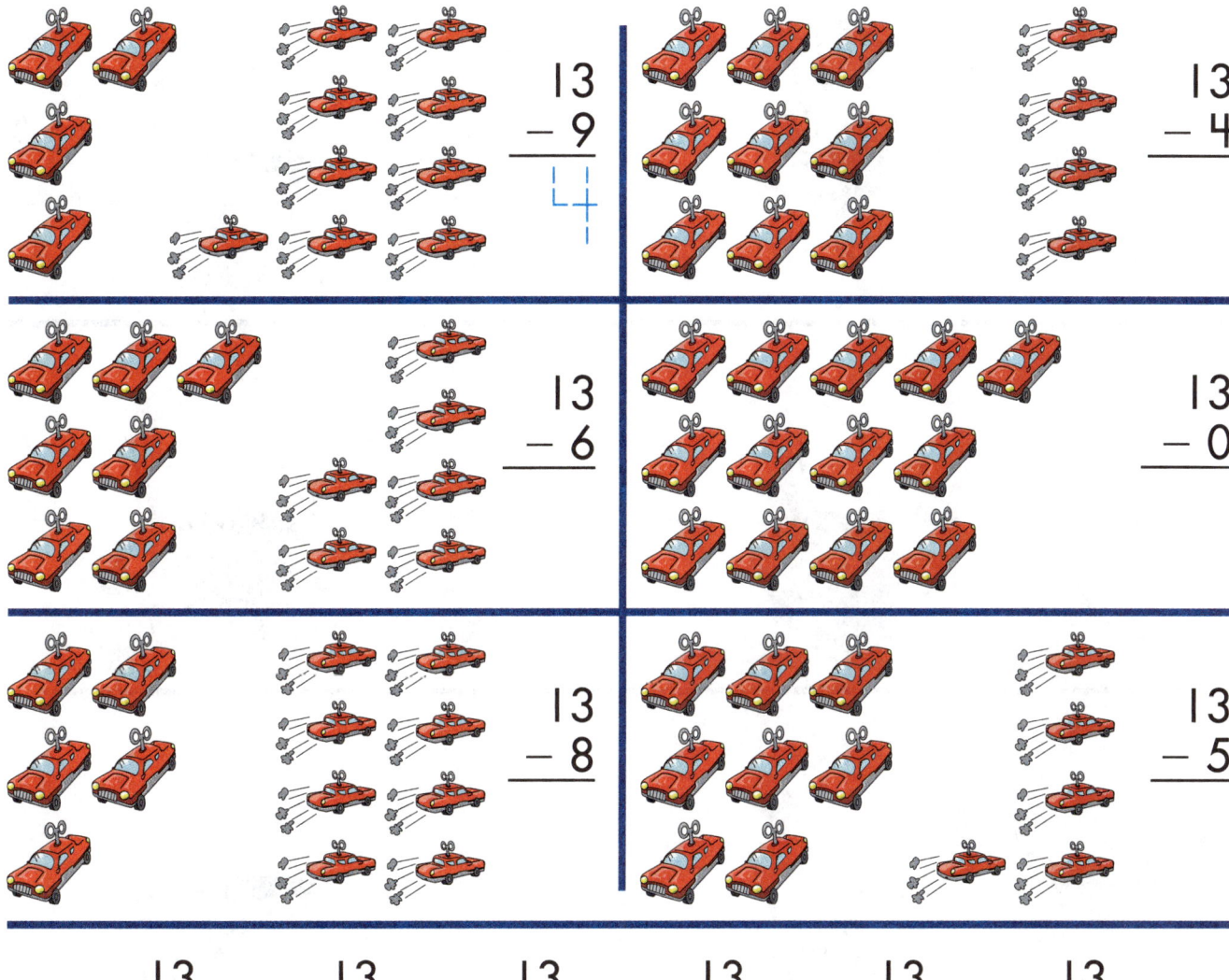

13 − 7 = _____   13 − 8 = _____   13 − 4 = _____

13 − 5 = _____   13 − 9 = _____   13 − 6 = _____

Spectrum Grade 1

Lesson 3.7 Adding to 14

Add.

   5
         +9
         14

   9
          +5

   8
          +6

   6
          +8

   7
          +7

   14
          + 0

```
  9      7      5      6      0      8
 +4     +8     +9     +8    +14     +6
```

5 + 8 = _____   7 + 7 = _____   6 + 8 = _____

Lesson 3.8 Subtracting from 14

Subtract.

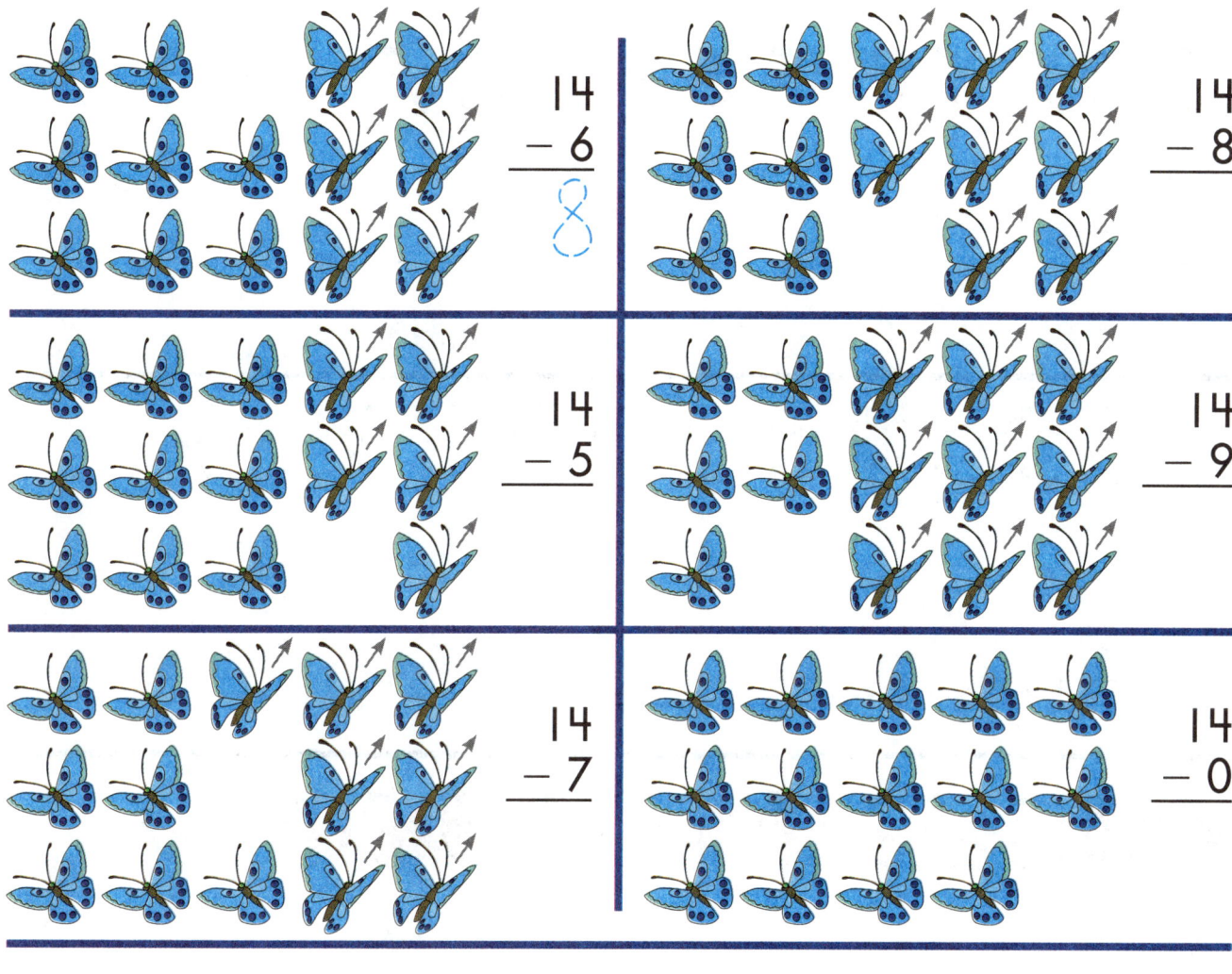

14 − 7 = _____   14 − 9 = _____   14 − 6 = _____

14 − 8 = _____   14 − 2 = _____   14 − 3 = _____

Lesson 3.9 Fact Families 11 through 15

Add or subtract.

```
  11          3         14         14
+  3        +11        - 3        -11
```

15 + 0 = _____   15 − 15 = _____

0 + 15 = _____   15 − 0 = _____

```
  12          1         13         13
+  1        +12        - 1        -12
```

3 + 12 = _____   15 − 3 = _____

12 + 3 = _____   15 − 12 = _____

Spectrum Grade 1

Lesson 3.10 Addition and Subtraction Facts through 15

Add.

$$\begin{array}{r}6\\+9\\\hline 15\end{array}\qquad$$

$$\begin{array}{r}9\\+6\\\hline 15\end{array}$$

| $\begin{array}{r}7\\+8\\\hline\end{array}$ | $\begin{array}{r}9\\+5\\\hline\end{array}$ | $\begin{array}{r}6\\+9\\\hline\end{array}$ | $\begin{array}{r}5\\+8\\\hline\end{array}$ | $\begin{array}{r}7\\+7\\\hline\end{array}$ | $\begin{array}{r}6\\+7\\\hline\end{array}$ |

| $\begin{array}{r}9\\+6\\\hline\end{array}$ | $\begin{array}{r}7\\+6\\\hline\end{array}$ | $\begin{array}{r}8\\+7\\\hline\end{array}$ | $\begin{array}{r}7\\+7\\\hline\end{array}$ | $\begin{array}{r}8\\+6\\\hline\end{array}$ | $\begin{array}{r}4\\+9\\\hline\end{array}$ |

Subtract.

$$\begin{array}{r}15\\-9\\\hline 6\end{array}\qquad$$

$$\begin{array}{r}15\\-6\\\hline 9\end{array}$$

| $\begin{array}{r}13\\-7\\\hline\end{array}$ | $\begin{array}{r}15\\-8\\\hline\end{array}$ | $\begin{array}{r}14\\-5\\\hline\end{array}$ | $\begin{array}{r}13\\-8\\\hline\end{array}$ | $\begin{array}{r}14\\-6\\\hline\end{array}$ | $\begin{array}{r}15\\-9\\\hline\end{array}$ |

| $\begin{array}{r}15\\-7\\\hline\end{array}$ | $\begin{array}{r}13\\-4\\\hline\end{array}$ | $\begin{array}{r}15\\-6\\\hline\end{array}$ | $\begin{array}{r}13\\-9\\\hline\end{array}$ | $\begin{array}{r}14\\-7\\\hline\end{array}$ | $\begin{array}{r}14\\-8\\\hline\end{array}$ |

Lesson 3.11 Fact Families 16 through 20

Add or subtract.

```
  14         3         17         17
+  3       +14        - 3        -14
```

2 + 16 = _____   16 + 2 = _____

18 − 2 = _____   18 − 16 = _____

```
  18         1         19         19
+  1       +18        - 1        -18
```

16 + 4 = _____   4 + 16 = _____

20 − 16 = _____   20 − 4 = _____

Lesson 3.12 Addition and Subtraction Facts through 16

Add.

 $\begin{array}{r}7\\+9\\\hline 16\end{array}$  $\begin{array}{r}9\\+7\\\hline 16\end{array}$

$\begin{array}{r}7\\+7\\\hline\end{array}$ $\begin{array}{r}8\\+8\\\hline\end{array}$ $\begin{array}{r}7\\+8\\\hline\end{array}$ $\begin{array}{r}9\\+7\\\hline\end{array}$ $\begin{array}{r}5\\+9\\\hline\end{array}$ $\begin{array}{r}9\\+6\\\hline\end{array}$

$\begin{array}{r}6\\+9\\\hline\end{array}$ $\begin{array}{r}6\\+8\\\hline\end{array}$ $\begin{array}{r}7\\+9\\\hline\end{array}$ $\begin{array}{r}9\\+5\\\hline\end{array}$ $\begin{array}{r}8\\+6\\\hline\end{array}$ $\begin{array}{r}8\\+7\\\hline\end{array}$

Subtract.

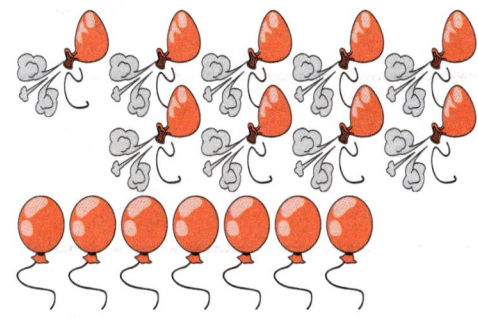 $\begin{array}{r}16\\-9\\\hline 7\end{array}$ 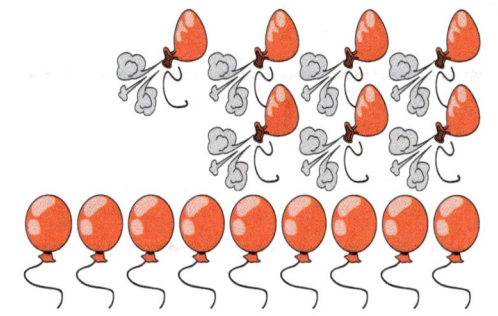 $\begin{array}{r}16\\-7\\\hline 9\end{array}$

$\begin{array}{r}15\\-7\\\hline\end{array}$ $\begin{array}{r}16\\-8\\\hline\end{array}$ $\begin{array}{r}14\\-9\\\hline\end{array}$ $\begin{array}{r}15\\-9\\\hline\end{array}$ $\begin{array}{r}14\\-7\\\hline\end{array}$ $\begin{array}{r}16\\-7\\\hline\end{array}$

$\begin{array}{r}15\\-6\\\hline\end{array}$ $\begin{array}{r}14\\-8\\\hline\end{array}$ $\begin{array}{r}16\\-9\\\hline\end{array}$ $\begin{array}{r}14\\-5\\\hline\end{array}$ $\begin{array}{r}15\\-8\\\hline\end{array}$ $\begin{array}{r}14\\-6\\\hline\end{array}$

Spectrum Grade 1

NAME _____

Lesson 3.13   Using Addition for Subtraction

Think addition for subtraction. Solve each problem.

17 − 3 = _____ | 3  + _____ = 17

20 − 5 = _____ | 5 + _____ = 20

19 − 5 = _____ | 5 + _____ = 19

18 − 1 = _____ | 1 + _____ = 18

15  − 4  = _____ | 4  + _____ = 15

14  − 2  = _____ | 2  + _____ = 14

16 − 1 = _____ | 1 + _____ = 16

20 − 6 = _____ | 6 + _____ = 20

13 − 0 = _____ | 0 + _____ = 13

Spectrum Grade 1

Lesson 3.14 Addition and Subtraction Facts through 18

Add.

  $\begin{array}{r}8\\+9\\\hline 17\end{array}$   $\begin{array}{r}9\\+9\\\hline 18\end{array}$

$\begin{array}{r}8\\+8\\\hline\end{array}$ $\begin{array}{r}9\\+8\\\hline\end{array}$ $\begin{array}{r}5\\+9\\\hline\end{array}$ $\begin{array}{r}7\\+8\\\hline\end{array}$ $\begin{array}{r}9\\+9\\\hline\end{array}$ $\begin{array}{r}8\\+6\\\hline\end{array}$

$\begin{array}{r}6\\+9\\\hline\end{array}$ $\begin{array}{r}7\\+7\\\hline\end{array}$ $\begin{array}{r}8\\+9\\\hline\end{array}$ $\begin{array}{r}8\\+7\\\hline\end{array}$ $\begin{array}{r}9\\+7\\\hline\end{array}$ $\begin{array}{r}9\\+6\\\hline\end{array}$

Subtract.

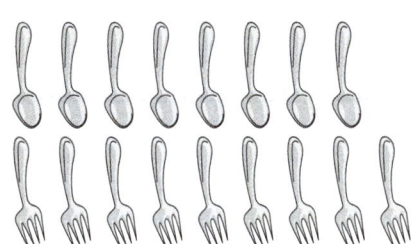 $\begin{array}{r}17\\-9\\\hline 8\end{array}$ $\begin{array}{r}17\\-8\\\hline 9\end{array}$ 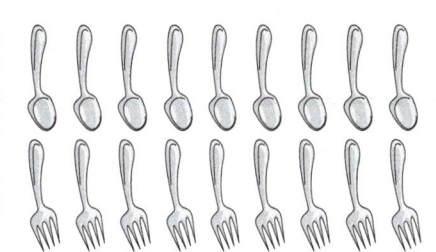 $\begin{array}{r}18\\-9\\\hline 9\end{array}$

$\begin{array}{r}15\\-8\\\hline\end{array}$ $\begin{array}{r}17\\-9\\\hline\end{array}$ $\begin{array}{r}14\\-7\\\hline\end{array}$ $\begin{array}{r}18\\-9\\\hline\end{array}$ $\begin{array}{r}16\\-7\\\hline\end{array}$ $\begin{array}{r}15\\-6\\\hline\end{array}$

$\begin{array}{r}17\\-8\\\hline\end{array}$ $\begin{array}{r}14\\-6\\\hline\end{array}$ $\begin{array}{r}16\\-9\\\hline\end{array}$ $\begin{array}{r}16\\-8\\\hline\end{array}$ $\begin{array}{r}15\\-7\\\hline\end{array}$ $\begin{array}{r}14\\-5\\\hline\end{array}$

Spectrum Grade 1

Lesson 3.15 Problem Solving

SHOW YOUR WORK

Solve each problem.

There are 17 ✏.

9 ✏ are broken.

How many ✏ are not broken? __8__

$$\begin{array}{r}17\\-9\\\hline 8\end{array}$$

There are 9 🐞.

9 more 🐞 come.

How many 🐞 are there? _____

Luisa caught 8 🐟.

She catches 9 more 🐟.

How many 🐟 did she catch in all? _____

There are 18 🐰.

9 🐰 run away.

How many 🐰 are left? _____

There are 17 🪏.

There are 8 🍴.

How many more 🪏 are there? _____

Spectrum Grade 1

Lesson 3.16 Using Addition for Subtraction

Think addition for subtraction. Solve each problem.

20  − 7  = _____ | 7  + _____ = 20

18 − 5 = _____ | 5 + _____ = 18

19 − 7 = _____ | 7 + _____ = 19

17 − 6 = _____ | 6 + _____ = 17

16  − 4 = _____ | 4 + _____ = 16

12  − 1  = _____ | 1  + _____ = 12

15  − 3  = _____ | 3  + _____ = 15

14  − 3  = _____ | 3  + _____ = 14

20 − 8 = _____ | 8 + _____ = 20

Spectrum Grade 1

Lesson 3.17 More- and Less-Than Facts 11 through 20

Add to find more than. Subtract to find less than.

How many is 2 more than 10 ? _____

What is 3 more than 16 ? _____

There are 5 less than 15 . How many are there? _____

What is 4 less than 14  ? _____

There are 4 more than 13 . How many  are there? _____

What is 2 less than 17  ? _____

How many is 1 less than 19 ? _____

How many is 5 more than 12 ? _____

There are 4 less than 20 . How many are there? _____

Chapter 4

NAME _____

Lesson 4.1 Adding 2-Digit and 1-Digit Numbers

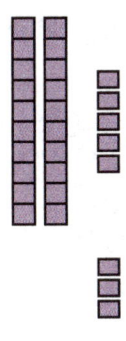

First add ones. Then, add tens.

```
  25        25         25
+  3      +  3       +  3
          ----        ----
            8       sum = 28
```

Add the ones.	Put the ones in the ones place. Put the ten in the tens place.	Add the tens.
38 8 +4 +4 ? 12 12 = 1 ten and 2 one	¹ 38 + 4 ---- 2	¹ 38 + 4 ---- sum = 42

Add.

```
  15        19        27        20        13
+  2      + 6       + 5       + 6       + 4
----      ----      ----      ----      ----


  38        22        29        47        14
+  8      + 6       + 3       + 2       + 1
----      ----      ----      ----      ----


  63        53        87        41        79
+  5      + 6       + 2       + 4       + 9
----      ----      ----      ----      ----
```

Spectrum Grade 1
57

Lesson 4.2 Adding Multiples of 10 to 2-Digit Numbers

6 tens and 8 ones plus 2 tens equals 8 tens and 8 ones.

```
  68
+ 20
-----
  88
```
↑
Only the tens place changes.

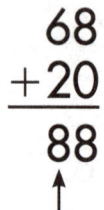 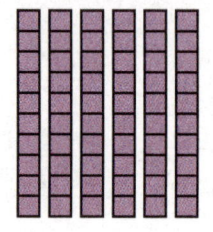 + 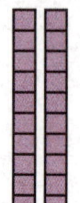 =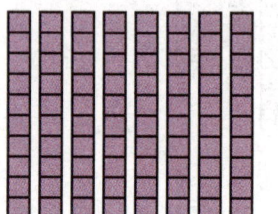

Add.

15	19	23	31	47
+10	+20	+20	+10	+20

13	29	17	11	60
+30	+40	+40	+50	+30

75	50	25	42	12
+10	+40	+70	+50	+80

18	12	20	59	15
+20	+80	+40	+20	+70

17	11	49	86	25
+40	+20	+30	+10	+70

Spectrum Grade 1

Lesson 4.3 Subtracting Multiples of 10

7 tens minus 2 tens equals 5 tens.

```
  70
- 20
  50
```
↑
Only the tens place changes.

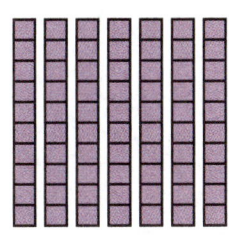 −  =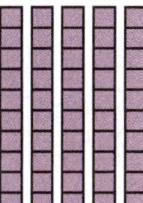

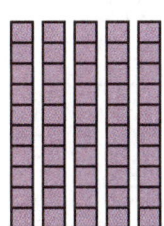 $\begin{array}{r} 50 \\ -10 \\ \hline \end{array}$ 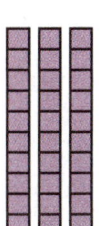 $\begin{array}{r} 30 \\ -10 \\ \hline \end{array}$

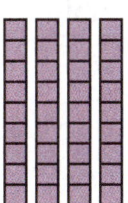 $\begin{array}{r} 40 \\ -30 \\ \hline \end{array}$ 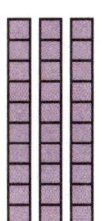 $\begin{array}{r} 30 \\ -20 \\ \hline \end{array}$

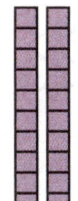 $\begin{array}{r} 20 \\ -10 \\ \hline \end{array}$ 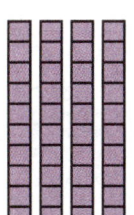 $\begin{array}{r} 40 \\ -20 \\ \hline \end{array}$

Lesson 4.4 Addition and Subtraction Practice through 100

Add.

9	9	16	27	28	37
+8	+7	+9	+8	+5	+7
17					

49	67	58	18	78	96
+9	+9	+7	+9	+6	+4

87	29	79	8	46	66
+6	+5	+6	+8	+8	+7

Subtract.

20	70	40	80	60	80
−10	−60	−20	−70	−10	−60

90	50	20	40	90	90
−80	−10	−20	−10	−40	−60

60	30	70	40	60	80
−60	−20	−10	−20	−50	−20

Lesson 4.5 Adding Three Numbers

Add the ones.   Add the tens.

```
 12  ▭▭▭▭▭▭▭▭▭▭ ▭▭       12         12
  4       ▭▭▭▭              4          4
 +3        ▭▭▭             +3         +3
 ──                        ──         ──
  9                         9   sum = 19
```

Add.

```
 10        11         4        15         2
  5         3         3         3         2
 +3        +5        +2        +2        +2
 ──        ──        ──        ──        ──


  2         8        12         2         1
  4         2         4         3         1
 +1        +1        +1        +3        +4
 ──        ──        ──        ──        ──


  5        15        13        11        12
  4         1         2         6         2
 +1        +1        +1        +2        +6
 ──        ──        ──        ──        ──
```

Spectrum Grade 1

Chapter 5

NAME _____

Lesson 5.1 Telling Time to the Hour

   11:00
eleven o'clock
Both clocks show the same time.

Write the time for each clock.

   __4__:__00__
__four__ o'clock

   ____:____
____ o'clock

   ____:____
____ o'clock

   ____:____
____ o'clock

   ____:____
____ o'clock

   ____:____
____ o'clock

   ____:____
____ o'clock

   ____:____
____ o'clock

Spectrum Grade 1

Lesson 5.1 Telling Time to the Hour

What time is it on the first clock?

Write this time on the second clock.

 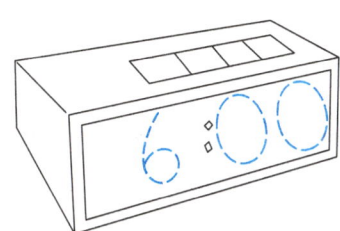  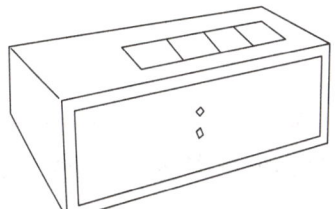

 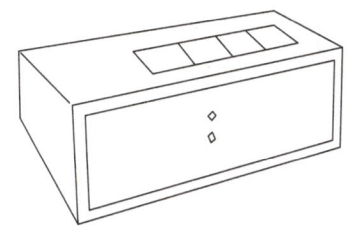  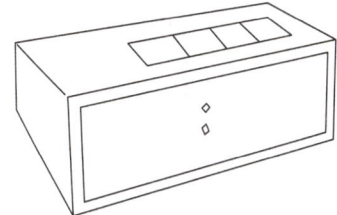

What time is it on the first clock?

Draw the hands to show this time on the second clock.

Spectrum Grade 1
63

Lesson 5.2 Telling Time to the Half Hour

3:00
three o'clock

3:30
three thirty

Write the time for each clock.

 1:30
one thirty

 ___:___
___ thirty

 ___:___
___ thirty

 ___:___
___ thirty

 ___:___
___ thirty

 ___:___
___ thirty

 ___:___
___ thirty

 ___:___
___ thirty

Lesson 5.2 Telling Time to the Half Hour

What time is it on the first clock?

Write this time on the second clock.

   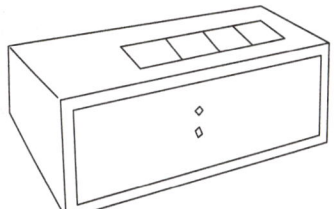

 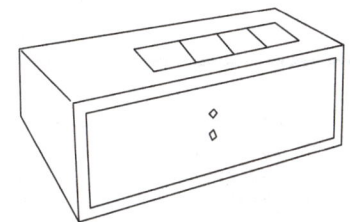  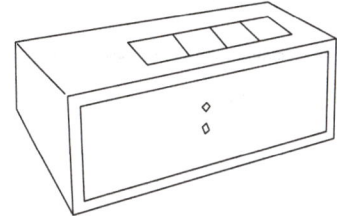

What time is it on the first clock?

Draw the hands to show this time on the second clock.

Spectrum Grade 1

Lesson 5.3 Ordering Objects

Number the objects as follows: 1– long, 2 – medium, 3 – short

  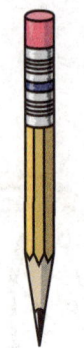   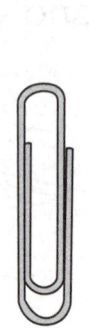 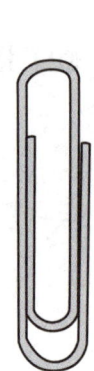 

_____   _____   _____   _____   _____   _____

_____   _____   _____   _____   _____   _____

 _____

 _____

 _____   _____   _____   _____

Spectrum Grade 1

Lesson 5.4 Comparing Lengths of Objects

Circle the object that is longer than the pencil in each row.

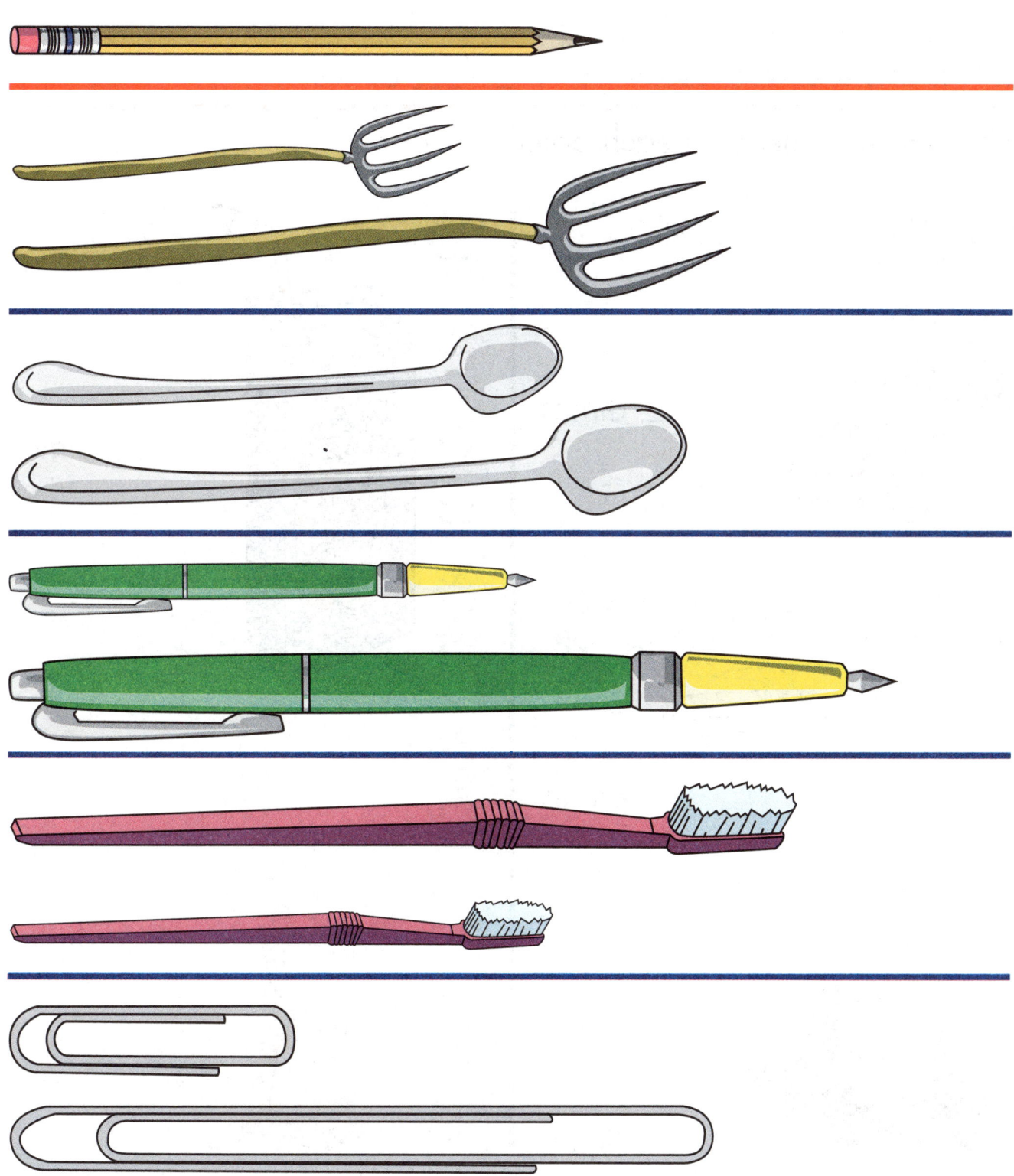

Spectrum Grade 1

Lesson 5.5 Measuring Length and Height

Use dimes to measure.

 _7_ dimes

Use dimes to measure each object.

 _____ dimes

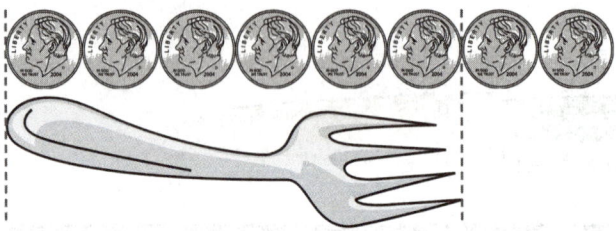 _____ dimes

 _____ dimes

 _____ dimes

 _____ dimes

Lesson 5.6 More or Fewer

Look at the picture graph.

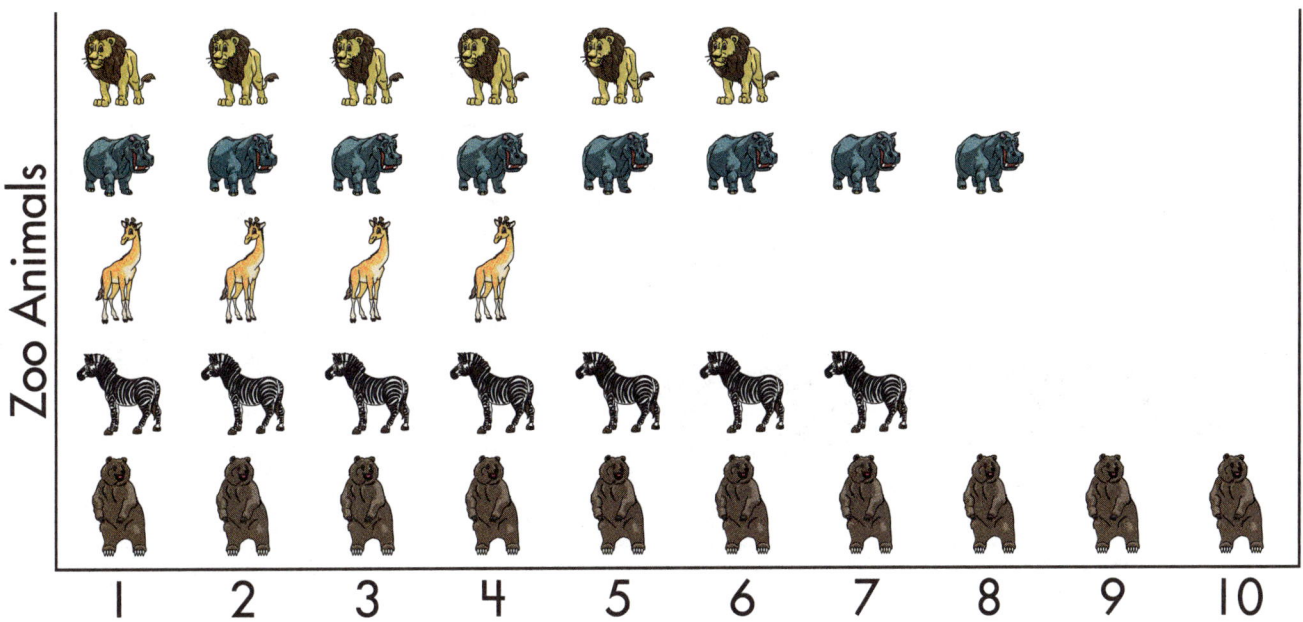

Circle the one that has more.

Circle the one that has fewer.

How many ? _____

How many ? _____

How many ? _____

How many ? _____

How many ? _____

NAME _____

Lesson 5.7 Greater Than, Less Than, and Equal To

Look at the picture graph.

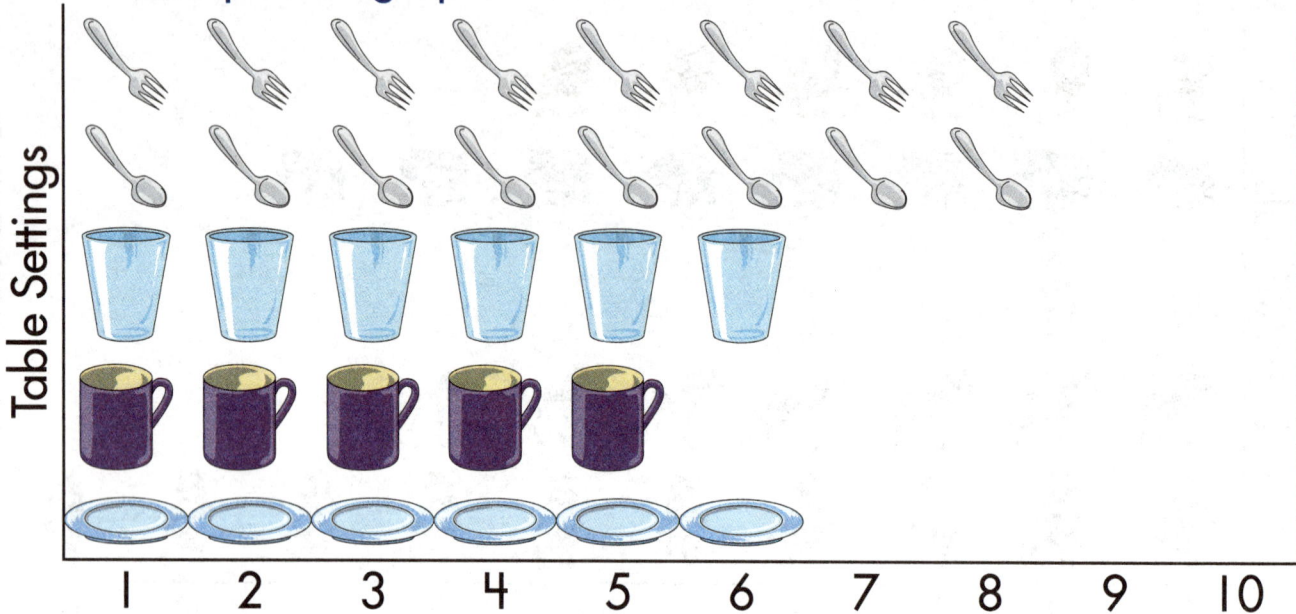

Circle the object that is greater than .

Circle the object that is less than .

Circle the object that is equal to .

Circle the object that is equal to .

Fill in the _____ with *greater than, less than,* or *equal to*.

 is ___less than___ .

 is _____ .

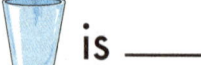 is _____ .

 is _____ .

Spectrum Grade 1

NAME _____

Lesson 5.8 Collecting Data

Make a food chart for one day. Show what you ate.

Fruit

Vegetable

Meat/Eggs/Fish

Bread/Cereal

Other Foods

Breakfast	
Lunch	
Dinner	
Snacks	

Use your food chart.

How many of each did you eat?

Fruit _____   Bread/Cereal _____

Vegetable _____   Other Foods _____

Meat/Eggs/Fish _____

What food did you eat the most? _____

At which meal did you eat the most? _____

What is your favorite food? _____

Spectrum Grade 1

Lesson 5.8 Collecting Data

Make a pet chart. Ask 20 people if they have a pet. Use tally marks to show what kind.

🐕	🐈	🐦	🐟	Other	None

Tally Marks
I = 1
II = 2
III = 3
IIII = 4
IIII̸ = 5

Use your pet chart. Write the number.

How many people have 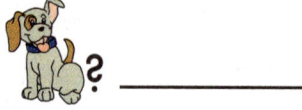 ? _____

How many people have  ? _____

How many people have  ? _____

How many people have  ? _____

How many people do not have a pet? _____

How many people have a pet that is not on the chart? _____

Complete.

Which pet is the favorite? _____

Which pet is the least favorite? _____

Chapter 6
Lesson 6.1 Identifying Shapes

NAME _____

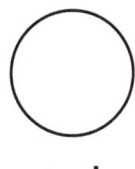 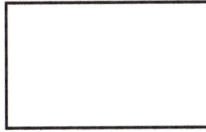  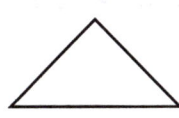

circle   rectangle   square   triangle

Write the letter C in all the circles.

Write the letter R in all the rectangles.

Write the letter S in all the squares.

Write the letter T in all the triangles.

 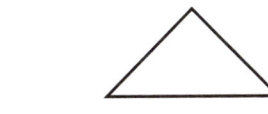  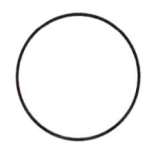

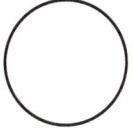  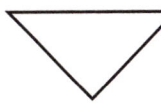 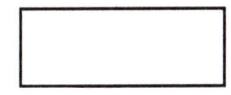

   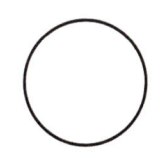

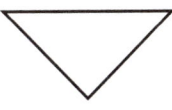 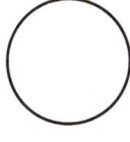 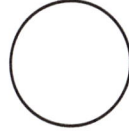 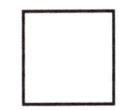

  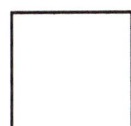

Spectrum Grade 1

Lesson 6.2 Drawing Shapes

NAME _____

Draw the shape.

Rectangle
It has 4 sides.

Circle
It is a closed curve.

Triangle
It has 3 sides.

Square
It has 4 sides.
The sides are the same length.

Triangle
It has 3 angles.

Rectangle
It has 4 sides.

Lesson 6.3 Finding Shapes

Write the name of each shape. Then, draw the shape.

   triangle

   _____

   _____

   _____

   _____

Spectrum Grade 1

Lesson 6.4 Composing 2-D Shapes

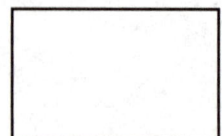  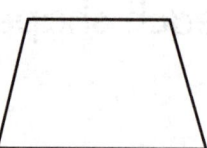 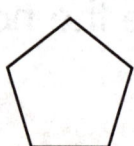

rectangle   square   trapezoid   pentagon

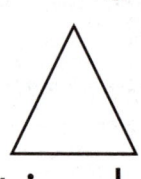  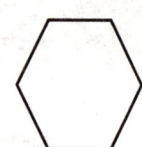

triangle   half circle   quarter circle   hexagon

Draw the shape you have when you put the following shapes together.

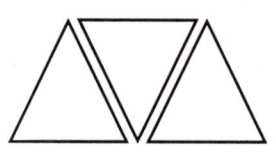   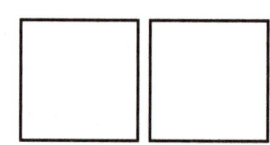

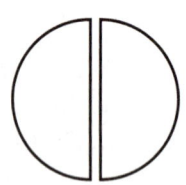   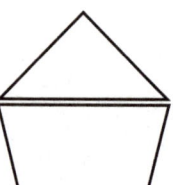

Lesson 6.5 Composing 3-D Shapes

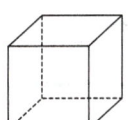 cube

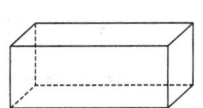 rectangular prism

 cone

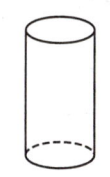 cylinder

Draw the shape you have when you put the following shapes together.

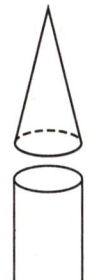

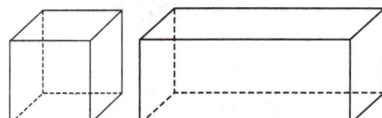

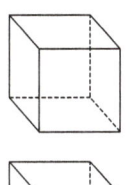

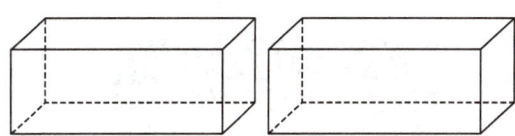

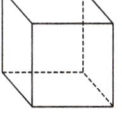

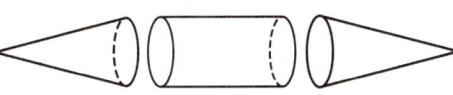

Spectrum Grade 1

Lesson 6.6 Partitioning Shapes

NAME _____

A shape can be divided into equal pieces. It can be divided into two equal pieces, three equal pieces, or four equal pieces.

Draw lines to show how you and a friend can equally share each item.

Draw lines to show how you and 2 friends can equally share each item.

 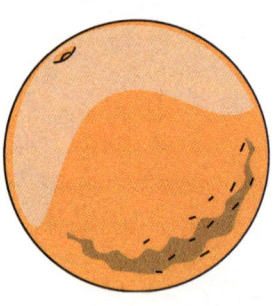

Draw lines to show how you and 3 friends can equally share each item.

Spectrum Grade 1
78

Lesson 6.7 One-Half and One-Fourth

One-half of the whole is shaded.

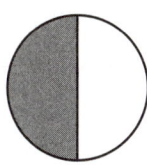

$\frac{1}{2}$ = **1** out of **2** equal parts

One-fourth of the whole is shaded.

$\frac{1}{4}$ = **1** out of **4** items in the set

Complete.

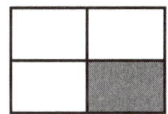

There are __4__ equal parts.
__1__ of the items is shaded.
__$\frac{1}{4}$__ of the whole is shaded.

There are ____ equal parts.
____ of the parts is shaded.
____ of the whole is shaded.

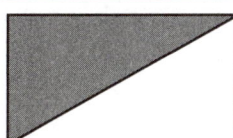

There are ____ equal parts.
____ of the parts is shaded.
____ of the whole is shaded.

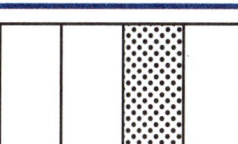

There are ____ equal parts.
____ of the parts has dots.
____ of the whole has dots.

Write the fraction that is shaded in words.

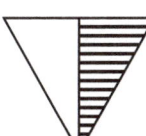

__One-half__ is shaded.

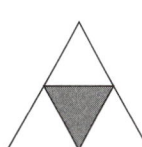

__One-fourth__ is shaded.

Spectrum Grade 1

NAME _____

Lesson 1.8 Questions

A **question** is an asking sentence. A question starts with a capital letter. It ends with a question mark.

(W)here is your house(?) (W)hat time is i(?) (D)o you have a ca(?)

Complete It

Complete each question with a question mark.

1. Who was the first U.S. president _____

2. Where was George Washington born _____

3. How long was he president _____

4. Did he live in the White House _____

5. What was Washington like as a boy _____

Try It

What if you could talk to George Washington? Write two questions you would ask him.

_____

_____

Spectrum Grade 1
97

Lesson 1.8 Questions

Match It

Read each statement about the White House. Read the questions in the box. Write the letter of the question that matches each statement.

> **A.** How many rooms does it have?
>
> **B.** Who was first to live in it?
>
> **C.** How many chefs work there?
>
> **D.** Who named the White House?

1. _____ Theodore Roosevelt named the White House.

2. _____ It has 132 rooms.

3. _____ Five chefs work at the White House.

4. _____ John Adams was first to live in it.

Tip: Questions often begin with words like **who, what, where, when, how,** and **why**.

Spectrum Grade 1

Lesson 1.9 Exclamations

An **exclamation** is a sentence that shows excitement. It can also show surprise. It starts with a capital letter. It ends with an exclamation point.

(I) need hel(p!) (We) won the gam(e!) (V)acation starts toda(y!)

Identify It

Read each pair of sentences. One sentence in each pair is a statement. The other sentence is an exclamation. Add the correct end marks.

1. I won the race _____

   Today is Monday _____

2. Finn is my best friend _____

   Finn found ten dollars _____

3. I have two sisters _____

   Something is out there _____

Try It

What is something exciting in your life? Write an exclamation on the line.

_____

Spectrum Grade 1
99

Lesson 1.9 Exclamations

Rewrite It

Rewrite each exclamation on the line. Remember, start with a capital. End with an exclamation point.

1. the dog got out

_____

2. don't knock over your cup

_____

3. lena's painting came in first place

_____

4. i lost my first tooth

_____

| Tip | Some exclamations are just one word. **Help! Wow! Great! Ouch!** |

Spectrum Grade 1

Lesson 1.10 Combining Sentences

Sometimes, two sentences can be made into one. Both sentences must tell about the same thing.

> Frogs live in the pond. Fish live in the pond.

Use the word **and** to join the parts of the sentence.

> Frogs **and** fish live in the pond.

Complete It
Read the sentences.
Fill in the missing words.

1. Max went to the fair. Li went to the fair.

   Max _____ Li went to the fair.

2. Mom rode the Ferris wheel. Dad rode the Ferris wheel.

   _____ and Dad rode the Ferris wheel.

3. The juice was cold. The ice cream was cold.

   The juice and _____ were cold.

4. Li played two games. Mom played two games.

   _____ and Mom played two games.

Spectrum Grade 1

Lesson 1.10 Combining Sentences

Identify It

Read the letter. Three pairs of sentences can be joined. Underline each pair.

June 12, 2014

Dear Ana,

Guess what? We went to the fair. I had fun. Marco had fun. We went on lots of rides. Tess stayed home. Jane stayed home. They are too little for the fair.

My ticket was lost. My money was lost. Don't worry, I was lucky. Marco found them. I left them in a bumper car. It was a great day. I love the fair.

Hope to see you soon!

Your friend,

Will

Chapter 2

NAME _____

Lesson 2.1 Capitalizing the First Word in a Sentence

A sentence always begins with a capital letter. This shows that a new sentence is starting.

Ⓦhat is your name?   Ⓣasha has two birds.   Ⓘ see the train!

Proof It

Look for the words that should be capitalized. Mark the letter with three lines below it (≡). Then, write the capital above it.

Example: S̲≡onya will wear her red dress.

bats are odd animals. They fly like birds. even so, they are not birds. Bats are mammals, like dogs and cats. most bats eat bugs. some eat fruit.

Bats sleep during the day. they are awake at night. They do not see well. They make a very high sound. the sound bounces off things. This tells bats where things are. it helps them get around.

Spectrum Grade 1
103

Lesson 2.1 Capitalizing the First Word in a Sentence

Rewrite It

Rewrite each sentence. Make sure to begin with a capital letter.

1. last week, a bat got in our house.

   _____

2. i didn't know what it was at first.

   _____

3. mom caught it and let it go outside.

   _____

4. that poor bat was scared!

   _____

5. i don't think he'll be back.

   _____

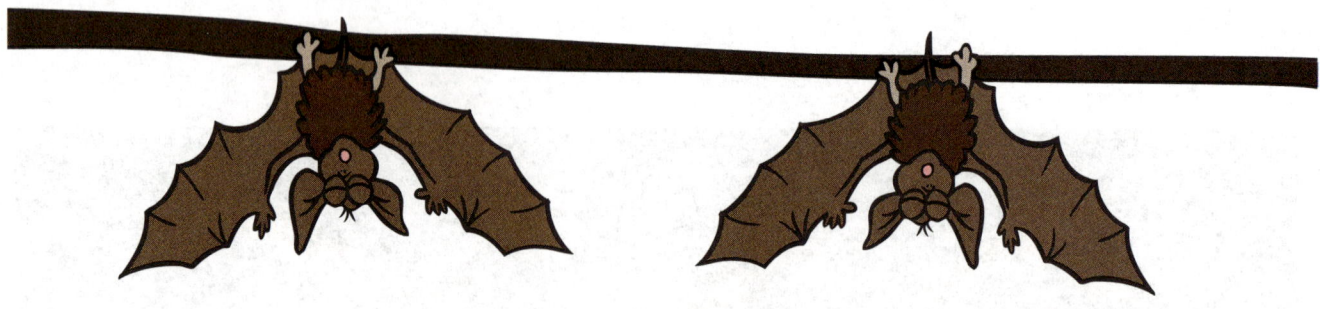

NAME _____

Lesson 2.2 Capitalizing the Pronoun I

The pronoun **I** is always capitalized. It can start a sentence. It can be in the middle of a sentence.

(**I**) like pears.   (**I**) will wear a jacket.   Min and (**I**) want to swing.

Proof It

Read the story. Each time you see the word **I**, make sure it is capitalized. If it is not, make three lines below it (≡). Then, write the capital above it.

Example: Lulu and i̲≡ went on a walk.   (with **I** written above)

   Last week, i went to the dentist. I was not nervous. i was just getting a check-up. My sister had a tooth pulled once. Grace and i were playing outside. She tripped and hit her mouth. I knew she needed help, so i called for Mom. Mom and i took Grace right to Dr. Cruz. i told him what happened. Then, Mom and I sat with Grace. She was so brave! Her lip was puffy, but she was okay. Grace and i will be more careful from now on!

Spectrum Grade 1
105

Lesson 2.2 Capitalizing the Pronoun I

Try It

Read each sentence below. Write the word **I** in the box. Fill in the other blank with a word that finishes the sentence.

1. ☐ like to eat _____.

2. _____ and ☐ play catch.

3. ☐ like the color _____ .

4. Each weekend, ☐ go _____ .

5. My _____ and ☐ like to read books together.

6. ☐ have a cool _____ .

Spectrum Grade 1
106

NAME _____

Lesson 2.3 Capitalizing Names

Names begin with a capital letter. A person's name starts with a capital letter. A pet's name starts with a capital letter, too.

My sister's name is **E**mma.   I have a cat named **S**ocks.

Match It

The child and pet in each picture need a name. Choose a set of names from the box. Write them next to the picture. Make sure you start each name with a capital letter.

| lily and lucky | carlos and coco | |
| ben and bubbles | greg and gus | stella and star |

_____ and _____

_____ and _____

_____ and _____

_____ and _____

_____ and _____

Spectrum Grade 1
107

Lesson 2.3 Capitalizing Names

Proof It

The names below do not start with a capital letter. Find each letter that should be a capital letter. Make three lines below it (≡). Then, write the capital letter above it.

1. luke, jay, and Leo are all sam's brothers.

2. Lu named the kittens bella and sassy.

3. Jack saw his friend ava at the park.

4. jess got to milk millie and Bonnie at the farm.

Try It

Write a sentence about two of your friends. Use their names in the sentence.

_____

_____

Spectrum Grade 1
108

Lesson 2.4 Capitalizing Place Names

Place names begin with a capital letter.

Danville, **K**entucky   **C**love **L**ibrary

Maple **S**treet   **J**ackson **S**chool

Venus   **J**apan

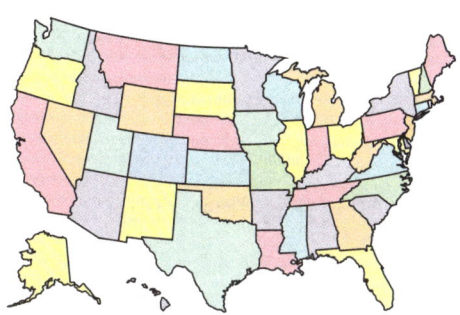

Proof It

The place names below do not start with a capital. Mark each letter that should be a capital with three lines below it (≡). Write the capital letter above it.

Example: We are going to m̲a̲ine this summer. (M above)

1. Ivan is moving to atlanta, georgia.

2. Do you think there is life on mars?

3. Addy goes to sandy brook elementary.

4. It snowed two feet in michigan!

5. Make a left turn on green road.

6. Lex swims at rock hill lake.

Spectrum Grade 1
109

Lesson 2.4 Capitalizing Place Names

Try It

Answer each question. Make sure to start each place name with a capital letter.

1. What is the name of your street?

   _____

2. What city were you born in?

   _____

3. What is a state you would like to visit?

   _____

4. What country do you live in?

   _____

5. What is the name of a place you go a lot? It could be a school. Maybe it is a store or a library.

   _____

Spectrum Grade 1

NAME _____

Lesson 2.5 Capitalizing Days and Months

The **days of the week** start with a capital letter.

Monday, **T**uesday, **W**ednesday, **T**hursday, **F**riday, **S**aturday, **S**unday

The **months of the year** start with a capital letter, too.

January, **F**ebruary, **M**arch, **A**pril, **M**ay, **J**une, **J**uly, **A**ugust, **S**eptember, **O**ctober, **N**ovember, **D**ecember

Solve It

Read each clue. Write the day of the week that matches it. Use the list above.

1. People like me a lot. I am the first day of the weekend.
   _____

2. I am the first weekday. My name starts with **m**. _____

3. You can find the word **sun** hiding in my name. _____

4. I am the last weekday. Here comes the weekend!
   _____

5. I come in the middle of the week. My name starts with **w**.
   _____

6. My name starts with **t**. I come near the end of the week.
   _____

7. My name starts with **t**, too. I come near the start of the week.
   _____

Spectrum Grade 1
111

Lesson 2.5 Capitalizing Days and Months

Complete It

Fill in the month in each sentence. Make sure to use a capital letter.

1. (june)   Julia's birthday is in _____.

2. (april)   Andy ate apples in _____.

3. (july)   Jake plays jacks in _____.

4. (may)   Mira met Matt in _____.

5. (october)   Olly saw an owl in _____.

6. (september)   Sam swam in _____.

Try It

When is your birthday? _____

What is today's date? Ask an adult if you are not sure.

_____

Spectrum Grade 1

Lesson 2.6 Periods

A **period** is an end mark. It comes at the end of a sentence.

I have a hole in my pants. Luis has a loose tooth.

Complete It

Each sentence below is missing a period. Add it and circle it.

Example: Turn on the lights.

1. Giant pandas are found in China

2. They live in the mountains

3. There are not many pandas left in the wild

4. Pandas have black rings around their eyes

5. They can weigh 250 pounds

6. Pandas eat bamboo

7. They get most of their water from bamboo

Try It

Look at the picture of the panda above. Write a sentence about it. Make sure it ends with a period.

_____

Lesson 2.6 Periods

Tip A capital letter can show you where a new sentence starts.

Proof It

The periods are missing in the paragraph. Add them and circle them.

Baby pandas are called cubs. A new baby is very small. It is about the size of a stick of butter. The cubs are not black and white. They are pink. A new cub looks more like a mouse than a bear. It has almost no hair.

A baby panda can not do much at first. The baby's eyes stay shut for 6 to 8 weeks. It takes a few months for a cub to learn to walk. Baby pandas need their moms, just like baby humans.

Spectrum Grade 1

Lesson 2.7 Question Marks

A **question mark** comes at the end of a question. It shows where the question ends.

Can you play checkers**?** Where is my red bow**?** Have you seen Erin**?**

Rewrite It
Rewrite each question. Make sure it starts with a capital letter and ends with a question mark.

1. where are you moving

   _____

2. have you packed yet

   _____

3. who will drive the moving van

   _____

4. what color is your new house

   _____

5. how far away is it

   _____

Lesson 2.7 Question Marks

Identify It

Read each pair of sentences. Add a period after each statement. Add a question mark after each question. Underline the word that tells you the sentence is a question.

1. What is your new address ?

   It is 811 Elm Street .

2. I can't find my roller skates .

   Have you seen them ?

3. What school do you go to ?

   I go to Shady Lane School .

4. Nick and Izzy live next door .

   Who lives in the blue house ?

5. Why are you moving ?

   My mom got a new job .

Spectrum Grade 1

Lesson 2.8 Exclamation Points

An **exclamation point** comes at the end of an exclamation. An exclamation is a sentence that shows excitement. It can also show surprise.

That's great news!   Look at the snake!   We won!

Identify It

Read each pair of sentences. Add a period after each statement. Add an exclamation point after each exclamation.

1. Today is Saturday_____

   It rained four inches today_____

2. Don't forget your umbrella_____

   Jon has a green umbrella_____

3. Watch out for that branch_____

   Dad will pick up the branches_____

4. Jaya did not step in the puddle_____

   My book fell in the puddle_____

Spectrum Grade 1
117

Lesson 2.8 Exclamation Points

Try It

Look at each picture. Write an exclamation to go with it. Begin with a capital letter. End with an exclamation point.

_____

_____

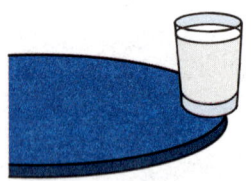

_____

_____

Lesson 2.9 Commas with Dates

A **comma** is a punctuation mark. In a date, it goes between the day and the year.

June 20,1973   October 6,2006   April 4,1866

If a comma is missing, use this mark (∧) to add it.

March 17∧2014

Proof It

Commas are missing from the dates below. Use this mark (∧) to add them.

1. John moved to New York on December 23 1982.

2. Aunt Keiko was born on February 19 1979.

3. Grandma and Grandpa got married on May 6 1960.

4. I met Jada on July 11 2008.

5. Riley's birthday is August 14 2004.

Try It

When were you born? Write the date on the line. _____

Ask a friend when he or she was born. Write the date on the line.

_____

Spectrum Grade 1
119

Lesson 2.9 Commas with Dates

Rewrite It

Rewrite each date. Use commas where they are needed.

1. January 5 1984 _____

2. November 18 2002 _____

3. May 23 1999 _____

4. February 9 2015 _____

5. July 31 1944 _____

6. September 12 1965 _____

7. April 29 1814 _____

Lesson 2.10 Commas with Cities and States

A **comma** is used between the name of a city and state.

Detroit, Michigan   Wilmington, Delaware   Portland, Oregon

Proof It

Add a comma between each city and state. Use this mark (∧) to add each comma.

1. You may have heard of Chicago Illinois.

2. You might know Dallas Texas.

3. Have you heard of Chicken Alaska?

4. Would you like to go to Bumble Bee Arizona?

5. How about Two Egg Florida?

6. Is it boring to live in Boring Maryland?

7. What is it like in Moon Virginia?

Spectrum Grade 1
121

Lesson 2.10 Commas with Cities and States

Complete It

Finish each sentence with a city and state from the box. Use commas where they are needed.

| Lima Ohio | Reno Nevada | Austin Texas |
| Macon Georgia | Portland Maine | Miami Florida |

1. Anton is moving to _____ .

2. In May, Izzy will go to _____ .

3. Lee's aunt lives in _____ .

4. It will take Cam two days to drive to _____ .

5. Dan found _____ on the map.

6. Jane has lived in _____ for 11 years.

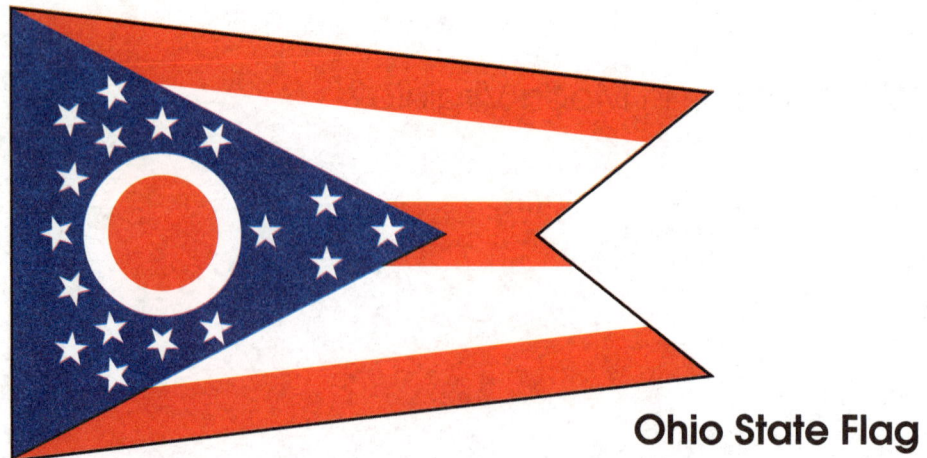

Ohio State Flag

Lesson 2.11 Apostrophes with Possessives

An **apostrophe plus s** (**'s**) shows that someone owns something.

    Keisha**'s** book   Meg**'s** brush   Cody**'s** train

Complete It

Add **'s** to each blank below. Make a line under the item each person owns.

1. Emma _____ drawing

2. Diego _____ pen

3. Mr. Stein _____ truck

4. Dante _____ leaf

5. Kat _____ frog

6. Jen _____ apple

Try It

Write a sentence about something a friend owns. Use **'s** to show what he or she owns.

_____

Lesson 2.11 Apostrophes with Possessives

Identify It

Read each pair of sentences. Make a check mark ✔ next to the one that is correct.

1. _____ Mia's hat

   _____ Mias hat

2. _____ Blakes bird'

   _____ Blake's bird

3. _____ Amad's boots

   _____ Amads boots

4. _____ Rosas muffin

   _____ Rosa's muffin

5. _____ Nicks snake'

   _____ Nick's snake

Spectrum Grade 1
124

Chapter 3

NAME _____

Lesson 3.1 Subject-Verb Agreement

When a sentence is about one person or thing, add **s** to the verb.

<u>Jim</u> drop**s** the ball.   <u>The leaf</u> blow**s** away.

When a sentence is about more than one person or thing, do not add **s**.

<u>The cats</u> look for mice.   <u>Jeff and Yoko</u> play the piano.

Match It

Draw a line to match each sentence to the correct ending.

1. Ms. Ito   grades the tests.

                               grade the tests.

2. The pencils   fall on the floor.

                               falls on the floor.

3. The bell   ring at 3:00.

                               rings at 3:00.

4. The girls   paints in the art room.

                               paint in the art room.

5. Caleb   sings after school.

                               sing after school.

Spectrum Grade 1
125

Lesson 3.1 Subject-Verb Agreement

Complete It

Circle the word that completes each sentence.

1. Max (puts, put) on his space suit.

2. He (slip, slips) on the boots.

3. The helmet (roll, rolls) across the floor.

4. Max and his dog (travel, travels) to outer space.

5. They (sees, see) Earth from far above.

6. Max's mom (calls, call) him home for dinner.

Lesson 3.2 Irregular Verbs: Am, Is, Are

The words **am**, **is**, and **are** are all verbs.

Use **am** with the word **I**.

    I **am** happy.   I **am** cold.

Use **is** with one person or thing.

    The balloon **is** red.   Seth **is** at the park.

Use **are** with more than one person or thing.

    The pens **are** in my desk.   The boys **are** inside.

Rewrite It

Each sentence below has the wrong verb. Rewrite it with the correct verb. Choose from **is**, **am**, or **are**.

1. The farmer am ready to milk the cows.

   _____

2. I is glad to help Bill.

   _____

3. The horse are brown and white.

   _____

4. The kids is by the pond.

   _____

NAME _____

Lesson 3.2 Irregular Verbs: Am, Is, Are

Complete It

Complete each sentence with the correct word from the box. Write it on the line.

1. is are   The pig _____ in the mud.

2. am are   I _____ sure I let the dog out.

3. is are   The ducks _____ with their babies.

4. am is   The cow _____ next to the fence.

5. are is   Farmer Bill and Henry _____ in the kitchen.

6. is are   The pony _____ six months old.

| Tip | Not all verbs are action verbs. **Am**, **is**, and **are** are not action verbs. Some other examples are **have**, **has**, **was**, and **were**. |

Spectrum Grade 1
128

Lesson 3.3 Past-Tense Verbs: **Was, Were**

The words **was** and **were** tell about something that happened in the past.

Use **was** with one person or thing.

    The bike **was** broken.   I **was** ready for dinner.

Use **were** with more than one person or thing.

    Amit and Liza **were** at the movies.   The books **were** in the car.

Proof It

Read each sentence. Check to see if the verbs **was** and **were** are correct. If you find a mistake, cross it out. Write the correct word above it.

Example: The worm ~~were~~ **was** under the leaf.

1. The parade were at 1:00.

2. The kids was excited to see it.

3. The balloons were red, yellow, and green.

4. The band were very loud.

5. Drew and Maggy was in the first float.

Spectrum Grade 1

Lesson 3.3 Past-Tense Verbs: Was, Were

Complete It

Fill in each blank with **was** or **were**.

1. The drums _____ in the middle of the parade.

2. It _____ a sunny day.

3. We _____ lucky it didn't rain.

4. Mom and Dad _____ on the sidewalk.

5. Nico _____ the leader.

6. At the end of the parade, we _____ tired!

Try It

Write a sentence telling how you felt on the first day of school. Use the verb **was** or **were**.

_____

NAME _____

Lesson 3.4 Past Tense: Add **ed**

Verbs in the **past tense** tell about things that already happened. Add **ed** to most verbs to tell about the past.

    It start**ed** to rain.   Henry knock**ed** on the door.

If a verb ends in **e**, just add **d**.

    live → lived   race → raced

Identify It

Circle the past-tense verb in each sentence.

1. The game started at 3:00.

2. A ball landed right next to me!

3. I picked it up.

4. The crowd cheered.

5. The game ended with a score of 4 to 3.

Try It

Write a sentence about something that happened last year. Use a verb that ends with **ed**.

_____

Spectrum Grade 1
131

Lesson 3.4 Past Tense: Add ed

Complete It

Complete each sentence with the verb in the box. Add **d** or **ed** to put it in the past tense.

1. look — The pitcher _____ at the batter.

2. wait — We _____ to see the hit.

3. race — The player _____ to first base.

4. jump — Number 3 _____ up to catch the ball.

5. sail — The ball _____ over the fence.

6. smile — I _____ at my brother.

7. want — We _____ to see a great game, and we did!

Lesson 3.5 Contractions with **Not**

A **contraction** is a way to join two words together. It is a shorter way to say something. An apostrophe (') takes the place of the missing letters.

Here are some contractions with **not**.

is not = isn't   are not = aren't

was not = wasn't   were not = weren't

does not = doesn't   did not = didn't

have not = haven't   can not = can't

Identify It

Read each sentence below. On the line, write a contraction for the underlined words.

1. I <u>can not</u> wait to go bowling. _____

2. I <u>have not</u> ever gone before. _____

3. Mom said it <u>is not</u> easy to knock over all the pins. _____

4. It <u>was not</u> hard to pick a ball. _____

5. There <u>were not</u> too many that fit my hand. _____

6. We <u>are not</u> going to be home by bedtime! _____

Spectrum Grade 1

Lesson 3.5 Contractions with Not

Match it

Draw a line to match each pair of words to its contraction.

Spectrum Grade 1

Lesson 3.6 Plurals with s

Plural means **more than one**. To make most nouns plural, just add **s**.

one hand → two hands   one plane → four planes
one tent → six tents   one hen → twelve hens

Solve It

Write the plural of each word on the line.
Then, circle the plurals in the puzzle.

bug _____   spider _____

beetle _____   cricket _____

wasp _____   ant _____

e	q	c	b	u	g	s
z	a	r	f	b	j	l
s	p	i	d	e	r	s
w	m	c	q	e	x	p
d	m	k	p	t	k	p
i	y	e	v	l	g	g
a	n	t	s	e	o	d
w	a	s	p	s	n	u

Spectrum Grade 1

Lesson 3.6 Plurals with s

Complete It

Add an **s** to each noun to make it plural.

1. Sanj found three ladybug____ .

2. Draw that moth with your marker____ .

3. Did you see the bee____ fly back to their hive?

4. Jose saw four slug____ in the garden.

5. Our dog____ get fleas every summer.

6. Watch out for tick____ in the woods!

7. Five inchworm____ crawled up the leaf.

Lesson 3.7 Irregular Plural Nouns

For some words, do not add **s** to make the plural. Instead, the whole word changes.

One	More Than One
goose	geese
man	men
woman	women
tooth	teeth
child	children
mouse	mice
foot	feet

Other words do not change at all. Use the same word for one and more than one.

one deer → five deer   one fish → ten fish
one sheep → three sheep   one moose → eight moose

Look at each picture. Circle the word that names the picture.

deers	deer	feet	foot
woman	women	children	child
gooses	geese	moose	mooses

Spectrum Grade 1
137

Lesson 3.7 Irregular Plural Nouns

Solve It

Look at each number and picture below. Fill in the missing word on the line. Choose from the words in the box.

mouse	men	fish
sheep	mice	teeth

4 (man) _____

6 (tooth) _____

1 (mouse) _____

50 (sheep) _____

17 (fish) _____

22 (mouse) _____

Spectrum Grade 1

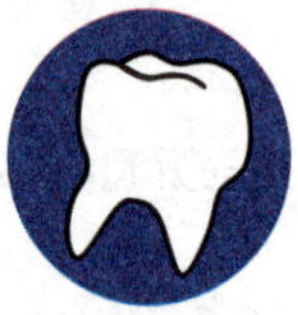

Lesson 3.8 Prefixes and Suffixes

A **prefix** is added to the beginning of a root word. It changes the word's meaning.

The prefix **un** means **not** or **opposite of**.
Example: **un**healthy = **not** healthy

The prefix **re** means **again**.
Example: **re**wash = wash **again**

A **suffix** is added to the end of a root word. It changes the word's meaning.

The suffix **er** means **one who**.
Example: bak**er** = one who bakes

The suffix **ed** means that something happened **in the past**. (Remember, if a word ends in **e**, just add **d**).

Example: Yesterday, Luis wash**ed** the dog.

Match It

On the line, write a word with a prefix to match each meaning.

1. read again= _____

2. opposite of dress= _____

3. not sure= _____

4. copy again= _____

5. told again= _____

6. not able= _____

7. fill again= _____

Spectrum Grade 1

Lesson 3.8 Prefixes and Suffixes

Complete It

Each **bold** word is missing a suffix. Add the suffix **er** or **ed**. Use the meaning of the sentence to decide which one to add.

1. Riley wants to be a **paint**_____ one day.

2. Kris **smile**_____ at the baby.

3. Lena **tuck**_____ her doll into bed.

4. The **catch**_____ stands behind home plate.

5. Mom handed a check to the **bank**_____.

Sort the words in the box. Write them under the correct headings.

reuse	liked	unhurt	farmer
singer	resell	fixed	unfair

Words with Prefixes   Words with Suffixes

_____   _____

_____   _____

_____   _____

_____   _____

Lesson 3.9 Pronouns **I** and **Me**

You use the words **I** and **me** to talk about yourself.

I like bananas.   Amit gave **me** a new book.

When you talk about yourself and another person, put them first.

Devon and I ride the bus.   Eli made dinner for **Dad and me**.

Identify It

Circle **I** or **me** for each sentence.

1. (I, me) take piano lessons on Tuesdays.

2. Ms. Hawk gave (I, me) a gold star today.

3. (I, me) like to sing and play.

4. Mom asked (I, me) to play for Aunt Clare.

5. Aunt Clare told (I, me) that I play very well.

6. (I, me) want to play in a recital this spring.

Spectrum Grade 1

Lesson 3.9 Pronouns **I** and **Me**

Complete It

Read the story. Write **I** or **me** in each blank to complete the sentences.

_____ play the violin. My grandma gave _____ one. It was hers. _____ have a picture of her playing it. She told _____ to practice every day.

My friend Avi and _____ take lessons. I started when _____ was three. He and _____ like to play together. He told _____ he wants to play the piano, too. My grandma says she can teach Avi and _____.

NAME _____

Lesson 3.10 Comparative Adjectives

Some adjectives are used to compare. Add **er** to an adjective to compare two things. Add **est** to compare three or more things.

Joe's dog is small.

Tasha's dog is small**er**.

Anton's dog is small**est**.

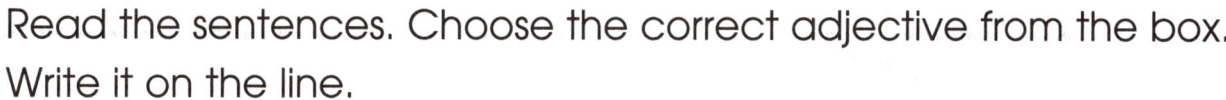

Identify It

Read the sentences. Choose the correct adjective from the box. Write it on the line.

1. | oldest older | Sami is the _____ of all her sisters.

2. | softer softest | Lola's pillow is _____ than mine.

3. | louder loudest | My alarm clock is _____ than yours.

4. | shorter shortest | Max has the _____ hair of all.

5. | slower slowest | Kiku's turtle is _____ than Alex's turtle.

Try It

Write two sentences. Compare two things in each sentence. Use these adjectives or one of your own: **harder, fastest, coldest, darker, youngest, longer**.

1. _____

2. _____

Spectrum Grade 1
143

Lesson 3.10 Comparative Adjectives

Complete It

Fill in the yellow spaces below with the correct adjective.

	newer	newest
warm	warmer	
hard		hardest
neat	neater	
	smarter	smartest
tall		tallest

Spectrum Grade 1

Lesson 3.11 Synonyms

Synonyms are words that mean the same or almost the same thing.

little, small   choose, pick   dad, father

Match It

Read each word. Find its synonym in the box. Write it in the matching mitten.

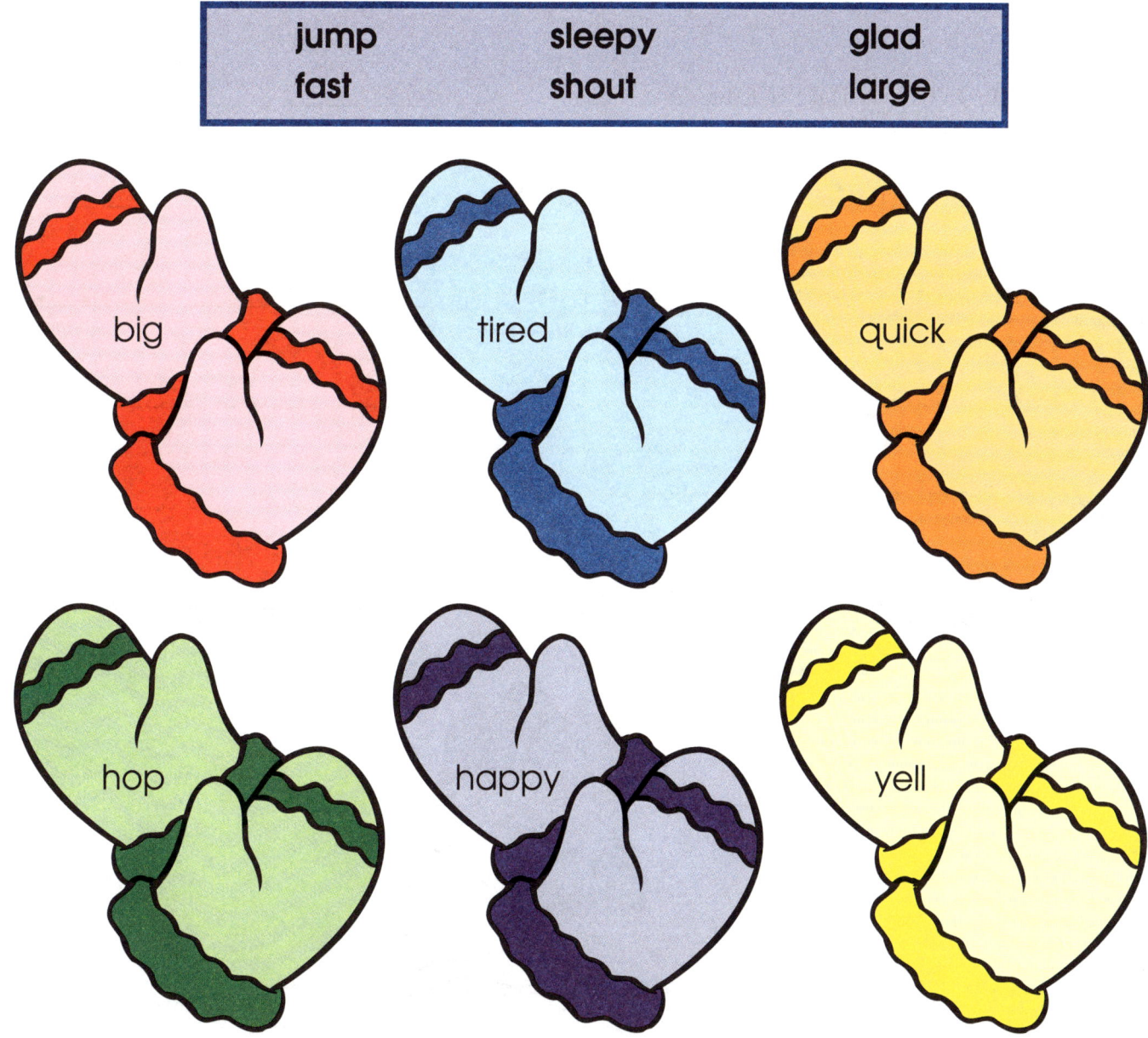

Lesson 3.11 Synonyms

Complete It

Read each sentence. Find a synonym in the box for the underlined word. Write the synonym on the line.

| toss | ship | small |
| begin | laughs | mother |

1. Please throw me that ball. _____

2. My mom made waffles this morning. _____

3. Don't start the movie without me. _____

4. Luke has a little dog. _____

5. The boat is white and blue. _____

6. Devi giggles at my jokes. _____

Lesson 3.12 Antonyms

Antonyms are words that are opposites.

hot, cold   black, white   old, young

Complete It

Fill in each blank with a word from the box.

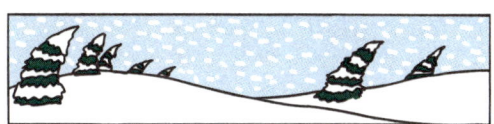

sad	front	go
night	down	full

1. The opposite of **day**  is _____ .

2. The opposite of **empty**  is _____ .

3. The opposite of **happy**  is _____ .

4. The opposite of **up**  is _____ .

5. The opposite of **stop**  is _____ .

6. The opposite of **back**  is _____ .

Lesson 3.12 Antonyms

Match It

Draw a line to match each word to its antonym.

right   last

first   tiny

new   loud

win   wrong

huge   out

in   old

quiet   lose

Try It

Draw a picture of two things that are opposites.

Lesson 3.13 Homophones

Homophones are words that sound the same. They have different spellings. They have different meanings, too.

to = toward					Throw it **to** me.

two = the number **2**				Nell has **two** cats.

too = also or very				Saki will come, **too**.

won = past tense of **win**			The Bears **won** the game!

one = the number **1**				**One** frog hopped away.

right = the opposite of left			Raise your **right** hand.

write = to put words on paper		Can you **write** your name?

Identify It
Underline the correct word to complete each sentence.

1. Jake bakes (won, one) cake.

2. Liam bakes (too, two) loaves of bread.

3. Reese can (write, right) down the recipes.

4. The flour is on the shelf on your (write, right).

5. Bella (won, one) first place in the bake-off!

Spectrum Grade 1

Lesson 3.13 Homophones

Proof It

Make a line through each incorrect homophone. Write the correct word above it.

1. Carter will bring the muffins two school.

2. Set up too tables for the bake sale.

3. Right down the names of all the pies.

4. Only won loaf of bread is left!

Try It

1. Write a sentence using the word **write**.

   _____

2. Write a sentence using the word **two**.

   _____

Spectrum Grade 1
150

Lesson 3.14 Multiple-Meaning Words

Some words are spelled the same but have different meanings.

Pat caught a **cold** last week.   **cold** = an illness

It is **cold** outside.   **cold** = chilly; not warm

Match It

Read each sentence. Think about how the word in **bold** is used. Draw a line to the picture that shows it.

1. Ivan swung the **bat.**

2. The **bat** looked for some bugs to eat for dinner.

3. Maddy can tell time on her new **watch.**

4. **Watch** the birds in the tree.

Lesson 3.14 Multiple-Meaning Words

Try It

Read each pair of sentences. Look at the meaning of the first word in **bold**. Then, write the word's other meaning.

1. Did you hear the phone **ring**?

   ring: the sound a phone makes

   Kelly tried on Mom's wedding **ring**.

   ring: _____

2. **Park** the car across the street.

   park: to drive a car into a space

   There are new swings at the **park**.

   park: _____

3. We **saw** Ruby at the store.

   saw: watched or looked at

   Use the **saw** to cut the log.

   saw: _____

Chapter 4

Lesson 4.1 Writer's Guide: Planning

Before you write, you need a plan. Start with a list of ideas. You may not use all of them. Still, you will find one or two great ideas.

Sit down with a pen and piece of paper. Make a list. What are some things you know about? What would you like to learn more about?

karate	trains
dolphins	rabbits
being a doctor	soccer

Once you pick your topic, you may need to learn more. You might look in a book. You can also use the Internet. Then, you can make an idea web. This puts your ideas in order.

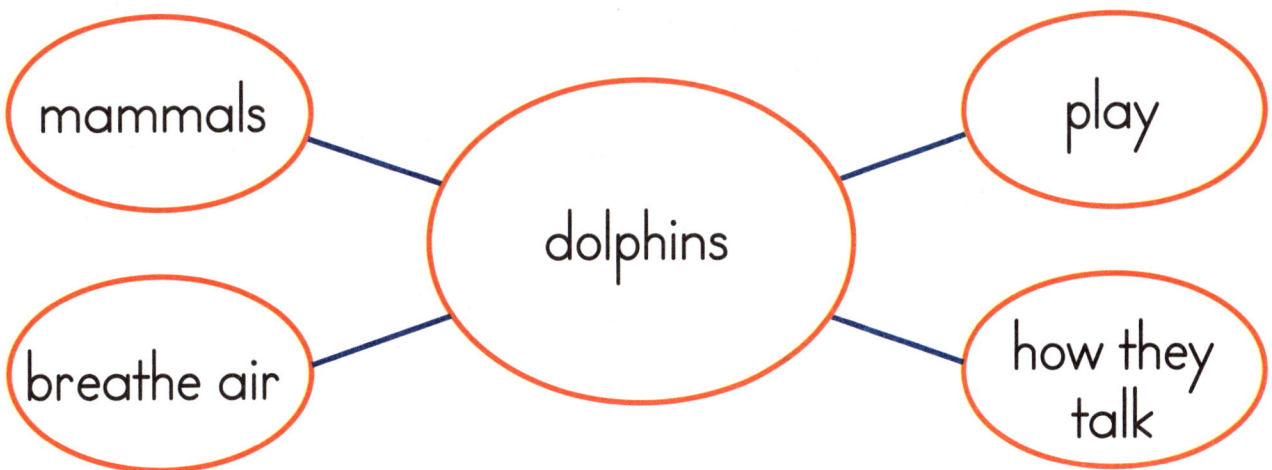

Try It

On a sheet of paper, make your own list of ideas. Which one do you like best? Make an idea web with the one you picked.

Spectrum Grade 1

Lesson 4.2 Writer's Guide: Writing

The next step is to start writing. Use your idea web to help you. Do not worry too much about mistakes. This is just a rough draft. You can edit your work later.

Dolphins

Dolphins are intresting animals. They look like fish. they are really mammals. Whales are mammals too. This means they have warm blood They also need to breathe air. They use a blowhole to breathe.

Dolphins like two play. They are also very smart They talk to each other with clicks and whistles. humans know a lot about dolphins.

Try It

Write a rough draft on another piece of paper. Use your idea web to help you get started.

Lesson 4.3 Writer's Guide: Revising

Now it is time to **revise**. Read your work again. You can even read it out loud. Look for:

- words or sentences that don't belong.
- places you need more information.

Dolphins

Dolphins are intresting animals. They look like fish. they are really mammals. ~~Whales are mammals too.~~ This means they have warm blood They also need to breathe air. They use a blowhole ^(on top of their head) to breathe.

Dolphins like two play. They are also very smart. They talk to each other with clicks and whistles. H̲humans know a lot about dolphins. ^(We still have a lot to learn.)

Try It

Look at the rough draft you wrote. How can you make it better? Mark your changes. If you need to, make a new copy of your writing.

NAME _____

Lesson 4.4 Writer's Guide: Proofreading

The next step is to look for mistakes. This is called **proofreading.** Ask yourself:

- Does each sentence start with a capital letter?
- Does each sentence end with a punctuation mark?
- Are all the words spelled correctly?

Proofreading Marks

∧ = add   Cal is seven y∧ers old.
⊙ = add a period   Saki has a blue hat⊙
≡ = make a letter a capital   Mr. h≡ale lives next door.

Dolphins

Dolphins are int∧eresting animals. They look like fish. T≡hey are really mammals. This means they have warm blood⊙They also need to breathe air. They use a blowhole on top of their head to breathe.

Dolphins like ~~two~~ to play. They are also very smart⊙ They talk to each other with clicks and whistles. Humans know a lot about dolphins. We still have a lot to learn.

Try It

Proofread your writing. Use the marks you have learned.

NAME _____

Lesson 4.5 Writer's Guide: Publishing

Make the changes you marked. Then, make a final, neat copy of your work. You are ready to publish! **Publishing** means sharing your work. There are lots of ways to share writing.

- **Read your writing out loud.** Ask your friends, family, or class to listen.
- Make a copy of your work. **Mail it** to someone you know.
- Read your work out loud. Ask a parent or teacher to **make a video** of it.
- Have an adult help you **put your work in an e-mail**. You can send it to family and friends.

Try It

Choose one of the ideas above. What did your friends and family say? What are some other ways to share your writing?

Spectrum Grade 1

Lesson 4.6 Writer's Guide: Writing a Friendly Letter

Start with **Dear** and the person's name, and a comma. Use capital letters.

Write the date in the right corner.

June 16, 2011

Dear Aunt Jen,

 Last week, we went to the beach. Dad and I went fishing. Guess what we saw? Three dolphins were playing! They jumped and splashed. It looked like they were smiling.

 Dad and I did not catch many fish. That's okay. The dolphins were the best part of the day.

 I hope you can visit soon. I miss you. Say hi to Uncle Nate.

Love,

Blake

The body of a letter is a place to share news.

A closing can be words like **Love**, **Yours Truly**, or **Your Friend**. A closing starts with a capital. Add a comma after the closing.

Sign your name. Remember to start it with a capital.

Try It

Write a letter to someone you know. Make sure to check for mistakes. Ask an adult to help you mail it. Maybe you will get a letter back!

SPECTRUM®

Reading

Little Duck

What is that sound?

What do you think Mama Duck hears?

Something is saying, "Quack, Quack!"

What do you think is making that sound?

That's a funny looking foot!

Whose foot do you think that belongs to?

Hey, it's Little Duck!

How do you think Little Duck feels?

Picture Interpretation and Reading (for all stories): Introduce students to Little Duck, a sweet duckling who is the focus of the following stories. Suggest that the students look at the pictures and talk about what is happening. Have the students relate what they see to their own lives and experiences. Be aware of the vocabulary levels and needs of the group. Key words may be reinforced or developed by writing them on the board as each picture/picture scenario is discussed. First, have students read the story silently by themselves. Help students with any unfamiliar words. Next, have students read the story orally. Discussion questions have been provided to serve as a discussion guide.

Spectrum Grade 1

NAME _____

Beautiful Beginnings

1.

_____   _____   _____

2.

_____   _____   _____

3.

  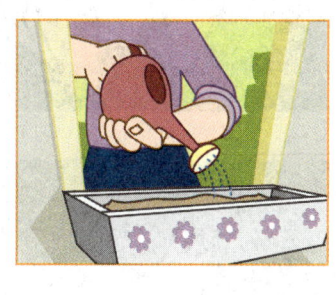

_____   _____   _____

Directions:
Beginning Consonants (1-2): Ask students to say each picture name aloud and listen to the beginning sound. Then, have them write the beginning letter on the line below the picture.
Sequence (3): Have students look at all the pictures. Ask them to write **1** below the event that would happen first, **2** below the event that would happen second, and **3** below the event that would happen third.

Spectrum Grade 1

Mama Duck

Mama Duck kisses Little Duck on the head. "Hello, Little Duck," she says.

Why does Mama Duck kiss Little Duck?

"Are you hungry, Little Duck?" asks Mama Duck.

Does Little Duck look hungry? How do you know?

Little Duck shakes his head up and down. Little Duck is hungry.

What does it mean when you shake your head up and down?

Mama Duck gives Little Duck some corn to eat.

What do you like to eat?

Beautiful Beginnings

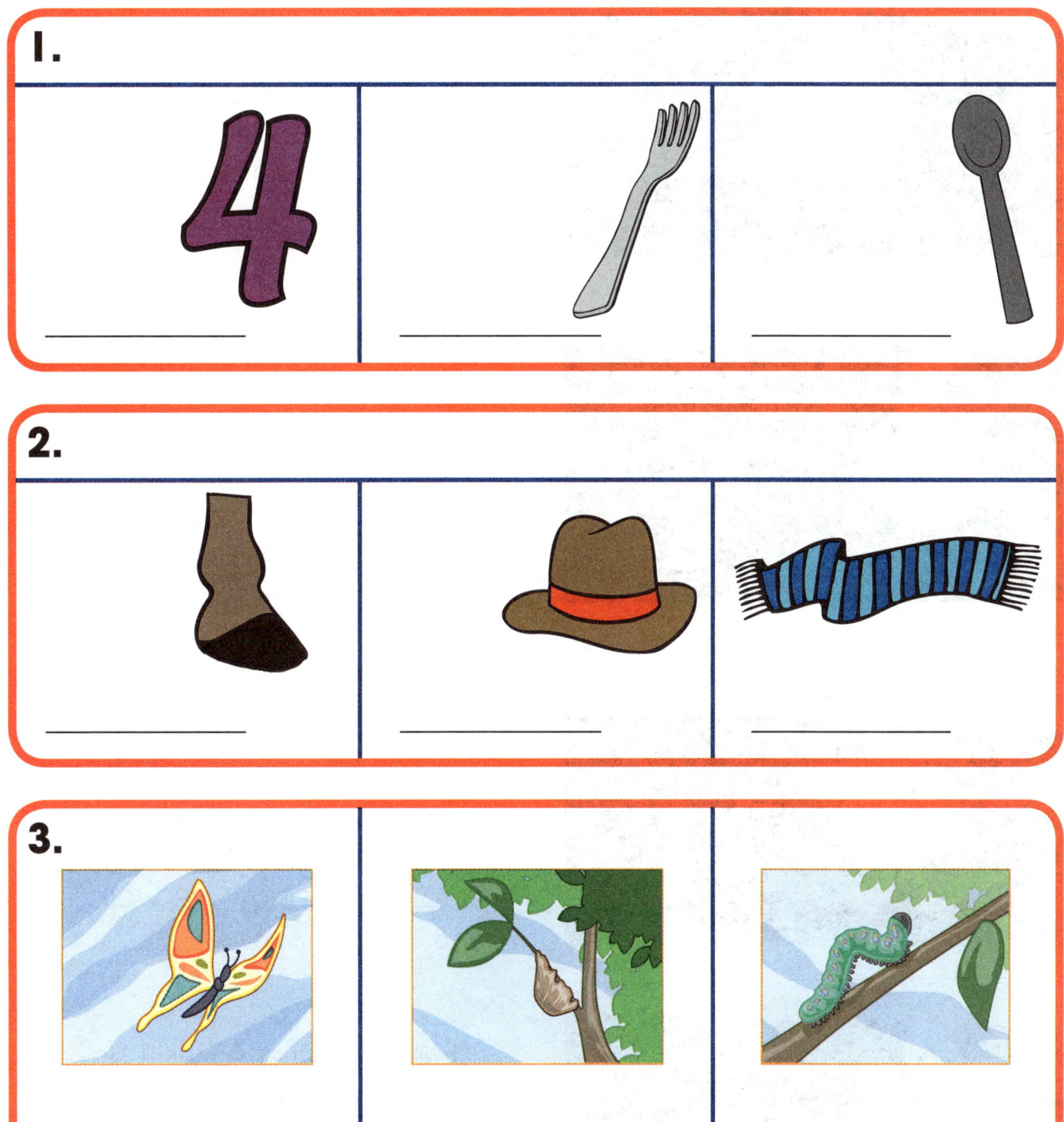

Directions:
Beginning Consonants (1-2): Ask students to say each picture name aloud and listen to the beginning sound. Then, have them write the beginning letter on the line below the picture.
Sequence (3): Have students look at all the pictures. Ask them to write **1** below the event that would happen first, **2** below the event that would happen second, and **3** below the event that would happen third.

Spectrum Grade 1
163

Wiggle-Waddle

Little Duck watches his mom walk. Mama Duck walks funny. She moves back and forth in a wiggle.

Why do you think Mama Duck walks that way?

Little Duck laughs. Why does his mom walk that way? Little Duck laughs and laughs.

Why is Little Duck laughing so hard?

"What's so funny, Little Duck?" asks Mama Duck. "Ducks waddle. This is how we walk."

What does it mean to waddle?

Little Duck tries to walk like Mama Duck. He wiggles. He waddles. He wiggle-waddles. Little Duck walks like a duck. Mama Duck is happy.

Why is Mama Duck happy? How do you think Little Duck feels?

NAME _____

Beautiful Beginnings

1.

_____   _____   _____

2.

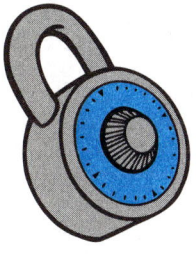  

_____   _____   _____

3.

_____   _____   _____

Directions:
Beginning Consonants (1-2): Ask students to say each picture name aloud and listen to the beginning sound. Then, have them write the beginning letter on the line below the picture.
Sequence (3): Have students look at all the pictures. Ask them to write **1** below the event that would happen first, **2** below the event that would happen second, and **3** below the event that would happen third.

Spectrum Grade 1

Dinnertime

Little Duck follows his mom to the pond. The pond is very large.

Where is Little Duck going? Why do you think he is going there?

Something moves in the pond. "What was that?" asks Little Duck.

What do you think moved in the pond?

"That's dinner!" says Mama Duck. Then, she quacks loudly.

What do you think will happen next?

A small fish jumps high out of the water and splashes Little Duck.

How do you think Little Duck feels getting splashed?

Beautiful Beginnings

1.

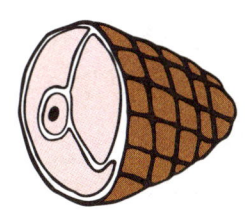  

_____   _____   _____

2.

_____   _____   _____

3.

ten   clap

snap   dime

chime   pen

four   score

Directions:
Beginning Consonants (1-2): Ask students to say each picture name aloud and listen to the beginning sound. Then, have them write the beginning letter on the line below the picture.
Rhyme Time (3): Have students draw lines connecting the words that rhyme.

Fish Is Not Dinner

Little Duck shakes the water off his soft feathers. "Who are you?" asks Little Duck.

Why do you think the fish splashes Little Duck?

"I am a fish, Little Duck. I swim in the pond. I am not dinner!"

How do you think the fish feels?

Mama Duck sees something. She waddles ahead. "Come along, Little Duck," she calls.

What do you think Mama Duck sees?

"Well, good-bye, fish," says Little Duck. "I guess we will eat something else for dinner."

Beautiful Beginnings

Directions:
Beginning Consonants (1-2): Ask students to say each picture name aloud and listen to the beginning sound. Then, have them write the beginning letter on the line below the picture.
Sequence (3): Have students look at all the pictures. Ask them to write **1** below the event that would happen first, **2** below the event that would happen second, and **3** below the event that would happen third.

Spectrum Grade 1
169

Make Way for Ducklings

Mama Duck walks to the edge of the road. Mama Duck turns her head both ways.

Why does Mama Duck do this?

"Cars make way for ducklings. Follow me, Little Duck," says Mama Duck.

What does Mama Duck mean?

Little Duck turns his head both ways like Mama Duck. Then, he follows Mama Duck across the road.

Why is it important to look both ways?

A boy sees the ducks crossing the road. He shouts, "Hey, make way for ducklings!" Little Duck crosses the road.

Do you think the boy is friendly? Why?

NAME _____

Beautiful Beginnings

1.

_____   _____   _____

2.

_____   _____   _____

3.

in   over   under   below

in   over   under   below

Directions:
Beginning Consonants (1-2): Ask students to say each picture name aloud and listen to the beginning sound. Then, have them write the beginning letter on the line below the picture.
Using the Pictures (3): Have students look at the pictures. Ask them to circle the word that describes where the cow is located.

A Feast

Little Duck follows Mama Duck up the hill. "Where are we going, Mama Duck?" asks Little Duck.

Where do you think they are going?

"We are going to find some dinner. When the sun sets, it is dinnertime for people and for ducks," says Mama Duck.

What time do you eat dinner?

"Was fish our dinner?" asks Little Duck.

Do you like to eat fish for dinner?

"Not tonight," answers Mama Duck. "Tonight, we have a feast!"

Do you know what a feast is?

Exceptional Endings and Blends

1.

2.

3.

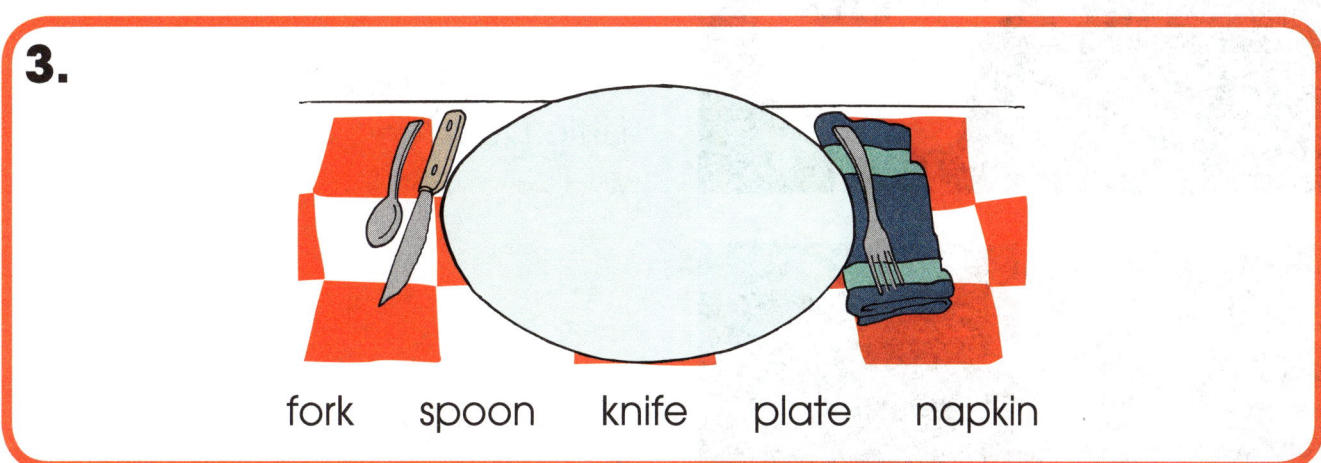

fork   spoon   knife   plate   napkin

Directions:
Ending Consonants (1): Ask students to say each picture name aloud and listen to the ending sound. Then, have them write the ending letter on the line below the picture.
Blends (2): Ask students to say each picture name aloud and listen to the beginning sound. Then, have them write the beginning blend on the line below the picture.
We Go Together (classification) (3): Have students circle the names of the three things that go together.

Spectrum Grade 1

Bread Crumbs

"What is a feast?" asks Little Duck.

Can feasts be different for different people?

"A feast is a large dinner. Tonight, we are eating something special," says Mama Duck.

What do you think Mama Duck and Little Duck will eat?

"Does it taste like fish?" asks Little Duck.

What would you like to eat at your own feast?

"It tastes better than fish. Tonight, we're having bread crumbs!" she says.

Would you like to eat bread crumbs? Why or why not?

Exceptional Endings and Blends

1.

____   ____   ____

2.

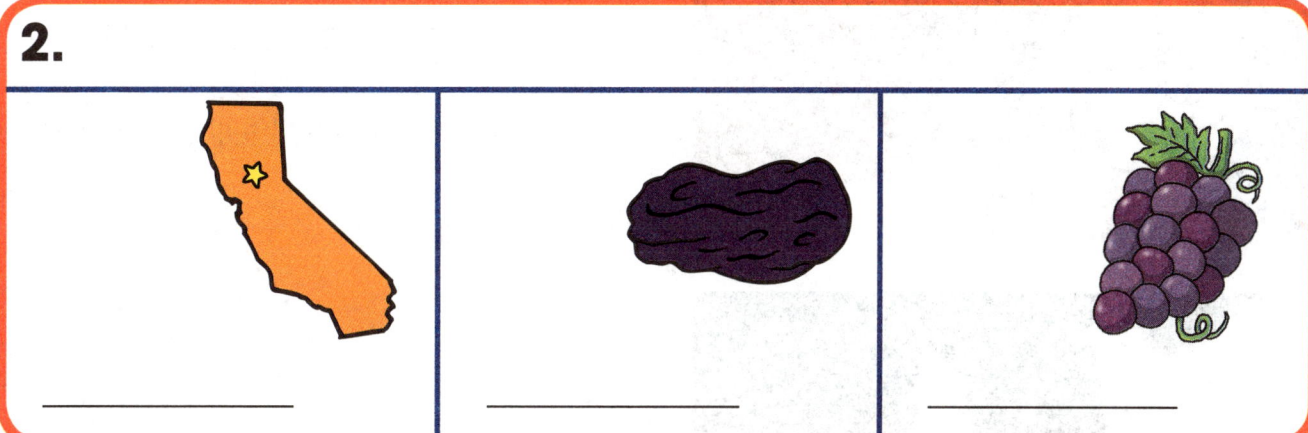

____   ____   ____

3.

nest   rock

dock   mother

brother   best

eight   date

Directions:
Ending Consonants (1): Ask students to say each picture name aloud and listen to the ending sound. Then, have them write the ending letter on the line below the picture.
Blends (2): Ask students to say each picture name aloud and listen to the beginning sound. Then, have them write the beginning blend on the line below the picture.
Rhyme Time (3): Have students draw lines connecting the words that rhyme.

Spectrum Grade 1
175

Little Duckling?

The boy opens the barn doors. He holds a large pail. The boy smiles at Mama Duck and Little Duck.

What do you think is inside the pail?

"Hello, Mama Duck and Little Duckling," says the boy. The boy reaches into a pail full of bread crumbs.

What do you think the boy will do next?

"Little Duckling?" thought Little Duck. "I am not Little Duckling, I am Little Duck."

Why is Little Duck upset?

The boy holds out his hand. "Come here, Little Duckling. I have some tasty bread crumbs for you."

What should Little Duck do?

Exceptional Endings and Blends

1.

_____

_____

_____

2.

_____

_____

_____

3. It is sharp.
It can hurt you.
Be careful when you use it.
What is it?

An eraser

A pair of scissors

A piece of paper

4. It is chewy.
You can blow bubbles with it.
What is it?

Ice cream

Gum

Soda

Directions:
Ending Consonants (1): Ask students to say each picture name aloud and listen to the ending sound. Then, have them write the ending letter on the line below the picture.
Blends (2): Ask students to say each picture name aloud and listen to the beginning sound. Then, have them write the beginning blend on the line below the picture.
Making Sense (3-4): Ask students to circle the answer that makes the most sense.

Quack, Quack, Quack

Little Duck did not come closer. He was not "Little Duckling." He was Little Duck. And he would not eat bread crumbs if he was not called the right name.

How is Little Duck behaving?

"What's the matter, Little Duckling?" asks the boy. The boy bends down and pats Little Duck's soft head.

Do you think Little Duck likes it when the boy pats his head? Why or why not?

"Wow. You have gotten big," says the boy. "I will call you Little Duck from now on."

Why do you think the boy will call him "Little Duck"?

Little Duck quacks three times. Then, he eats bread crumbs from the boy's hand.

How does Little Duck feel now? How do you know?

NAME _____

Endless Endings

1.

_____   _____   _____

2. school   student   teacher   doctor

3. bird   frog    human   dog

4. circle    two   eight   six

5.

There are four birds.
There are five birds.

6.

There are 5 – 2 toads.
There are 1 + 3 toads.

Directions:
Ending Consonants (1): Ask students to say each picture name aloud and listen to the ending sound. Then, have them write the ending letter on the line below the picture.
Classification (2-4): Have students look at all four pictures or words in each row and then circle the three that belong together.
Using the Pictures (5-6): Have students look at the pictures in each box. Then, have them circle the sentence that describes the picture.

Spectrum Grade 1
179

Brrr!

Little Duck dips his foot into the pond. The water is so cold. "Brrr!" says Little Duck.

Have you ever felt cold water like Little Duck?

Mama Duck laughs and says, "It is not cold, Little Duck. Plus, you're a duck. Our feathers keep us warm in cold water."

How do people keep warm when it is cold?

Little Duck wades into the water. The water is cold, but nice. Maybe Little Duck will see the fish again.

Why does Little Duck want to see fish again?

Something strange is in the water. "Mama Duck, what is that?" asks Little Duck.

What do you think is in the water?

NAME _____

More Endings

1.

_____

_____

_____

2.

_____

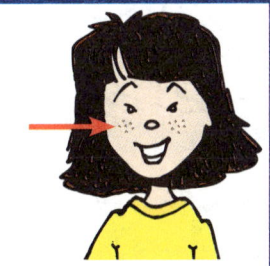
_____

_____

3. Write a sentence that includes one of the words above in #2.

_____

_____

Directions:
Ending Consonants (1): Ask students to say each picture name aloud and listen to the ending sound. Then, have them write the ending letter on the line below the picture.
Blends (2): Ask students to say each picture name aloud and listen to the beginning sound. Then, have them write the beginning blend on the line below the picture.
Writing Time (3): See directions in #3.

New Friend

Little Duck and his mom swim closer to the strange thing. A girl duck pops up from under the water.

Have you ever felt water like Little Duck?

"Wow, that was fun!" says the girl duck. "I love diving in the water."

Do you think she is looking for something? What?

"You don't think it is too cold?" asks Little Duck.

"No," she says. "The water is just right. My name is Matilda. What's yours?"

"My name is Little Duck."

What do you think happens next?

NAME _____

Keep on Blending

1.

2.

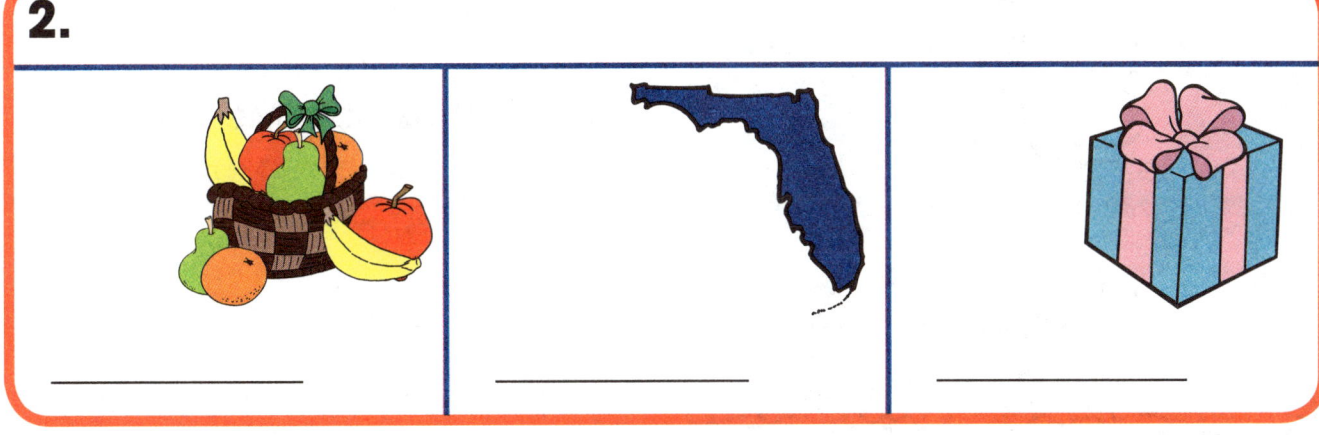

3.

Directions:
Ending Consonants (1): Ask students to say each picture name aloud and listen to the ending sound. Then, have them write the ending letter on the line below the picture.
Blends (2): Ask students to say each picture name aloud and listen to the beginning sound. Then, have them write the beginning blend on the line below the picture.
Sequence (3): Have students look at all three pictures. Ask them to write **1** below the event that would happen first, **2** below the event that would happen second, and **3** below the event that would happen third.

Spectrum Grade 1
183

Snails Away!

"Do you want to dive for snails, Little Duck?" asks Matilda. "They live at the bottom of the pond."

Do you think Little Duck will say yes or no? Why?

"I don't know how to dive," says Little Duck.

"Sure you do. All ducks know how to dive," says Matilda.

Do you think Little Duck will know how to dive? Why?

"I'll try," says Little Duck, and he dives into the water. It is fun underwater. But Little Duck doesn't see any snails.

What other things might Little Duck see underwater?

Little Duck and Matilda come up for air. They didn't catch even one snail. "Well," says Matilda, "there is only one thing to be done."

What do you think Little Duck and Matilda will do next?

Is the End in Sight?

1.

      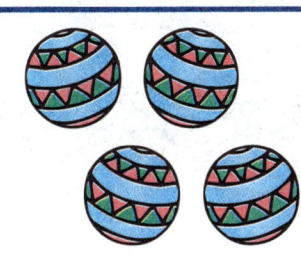

_____   _____   _____

2.

   _____

_____   _____   _____

3.

seven   brick

trick   eleven

sneak   leak

treat   beat

Directions:
Ending Consonants (1): Ask students to say each picture name aloud and listen to the ending sound. Then, have them write the ending letter on the line below the picture.
Blends (2): Ask students to say each picture name aloud and listen to the beginning sound. Then, have them write the beginning blend on the line below the picture.
Rhyme Time (3): Have students draw lines connecting the words that rhyme.

Spectrum Grade 1

Little Duck and Matilda Go to the Farm

Little Duck and Matilda waddle along the side of the road. "Where are we going?" asks Little Duck.

Where do you think they are going?

"We are going to the farm on the hill. The farmer throws away old corn. He throws away stale bread. He throws away grass clippings," says Matilda.

Would you want to eat stale bread? Why or why not?

"What do we do now?" asks Little Duck.

"We will take some of this home with us," says Matilda.

"We are going to make some duck soup," says Matilda.

"Does duck soup taste good?" asks Little Duck.

"Duck soup tastes very good. You'll see," says Matilda.

Do you think duck soup will taste good? Who is telling the story: Matilda, Little Duck, or the author?

NAME _____

Valuable Vowels

1.

_____   _____   _____

2.

_____   _____   _____

3.

_____

Directions:
Long Vowels (1): Have students name each picture. Then, have them write the long vowel on the line provided.
Dynamite Digraphs (2): Review the **ch** digraph. Have students name each picture. Ask them to write **ch** below each picture that begins with the **ch** sound.
One or More (3): Have students look at all four pictures. Ask them to identify the pictures with only one (singular) object. Tell students to write down their answers.

Spectrum Grade 1

Duck Soup

Matilda and Little Duck sit by the edge of the pond. "What is in duck soup?" asks Little Duck.

Would you want to eat duck soup? Why or why not?

"Close your eyes and take a guess," says Matilda. "Duck soup is the best soup in the whole world."

What do you think Little Duck tastes?

"I taste corn," says Little Duck, "and I taste bread crumbs. And I taste something green."

What do you think Little Duck tastes that is green?

"Good guess, Little Duck," says Matilda. "Duck soup is made of corn, water, bread crumbs, and grass. Yummy for ducks."

Do you think you would like to eat a bowl of duck soup?

Vowels

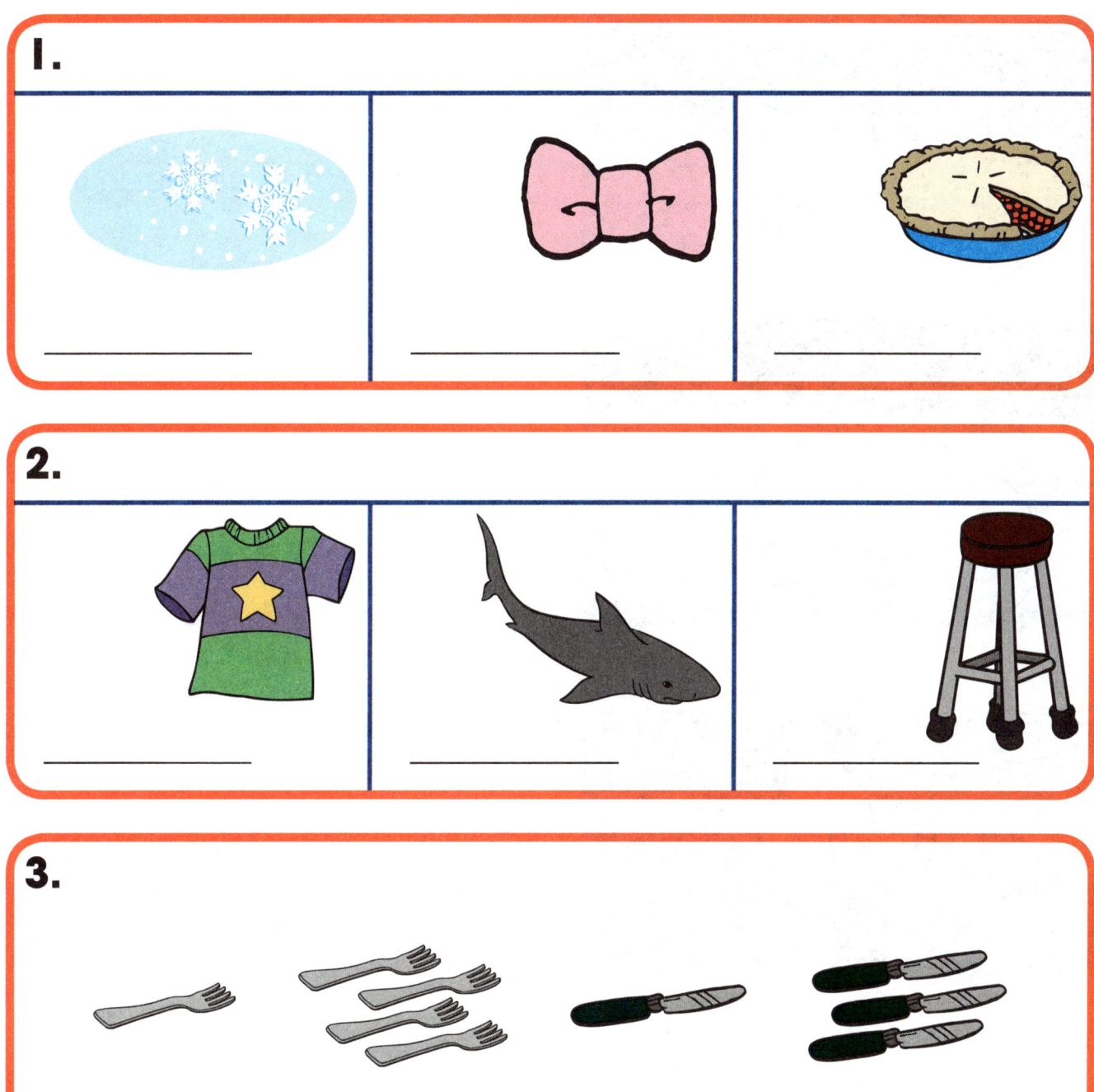

Directions:
Long Vowels (1): Have students name each picture. Then, have them write the long vowel on the line provided.
Dynamite Digraphs (2): Review the **sh** digraph. Have students name each picture. Ask them to write **sh** below each picture that begins with the **sh** sound.
One or More (3): Have students look at all four pictures. Ask them to identify the pictures with only one (singular) object. Tell students to write down their answers.

Spectrum Grade 1

Little Duck Dives

Little Duck swims by himself in the pond. Every day, he tries to dive deeper and deeper in the pond.

What do you like to practice?

Little Duck wants to find a snail to give to Matilda. One day, he sees something at the bottom of the pond.

What do you think Little Duck sees?

Little Duck swims deeper and deeper to the pond bottom. Something is shiny. It is not a snail.

What do you think is at the bottom?

"What is this?" says Little Duck. He carries a penny in his beak and puts it in the grass.

What do you think Little Duck will do with the penny he found?

Dynamite Digraphs

Directions:
Dynamite Digraphs (1): Review the **th** digraph. Have students name each picture. Ask them to write **th** below each picture that begins with the **th** sound.
Long Vowels (2): Have students name each picture. Then, ask them to write the long vowel on the line provided.
Double Time: Blends and Digraphs (3): Write two words that start with a blend and end with a consonant digraph. Example: French.

Spectrum Grade 1

What to Do with a Penny

"What should we do with the penny?" asks Little Duck. "Should we add it to the duck soup? Maybe it will taste good with the corn, bread crumbs, and grass?"

What do you think Matilda and Little Duck should do with the penny?

"I don't think you can eat a penny," says Matilda. "Why don't we ask your mom if she knows what to do with it?"

What do you think Mama Duck will say?

Little Duck and Matilda waddle over to Mama Duck. "Mama Duck, what should we do with a penny?" asks Little Duck.

What are some things you would do with a penny?

"Well, you should throw the penny back into the pond and make a wish," says Mama Duck.

Would you want to throw the penny back and make a wish?

Dynamite Digraphs

1.

  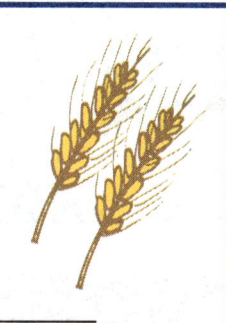

_____   _____   _____

2.

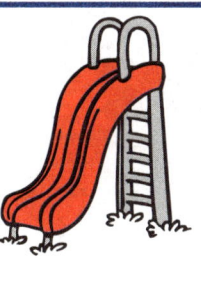  

_____   _____   _____

3.

_____ The crowd cheers.

_____ The batter comes to the plate.

_____ The batter strikes out.

Directions:
Dynamite Digraphs (1): Review the **wh** digraph. Have students name each picture. Ask them to write **wh** below each picture that begins with the **wh** sound.
Vowels (2): Have students name each picture. Then, ask students to write the vowel on the line provided.
Sequence (3): Have students read all three sentences. Ask them to write **1** next to the event that would happen first, **2** next to the event that would happen second, and **3** next to the event that would happen third.

Spectrum Grade 1

Make a Wish, Little Duck

"What should I wish for?" asks Little Duck. "I already have everything I want. I have the best Mama Duck, and I have a best friend."

What would you wish for?

"Well, isn't there anything else you want, Little Duck?" asks Mama Duck.

What could Little Duck wish for?

"I guess I wish I could fly like the big ducks in the sky," says Little Duck. He throws the penny back in the pond.

Do you think Little Duck makes a good wish? How come?

"But Little Duck, your wish has already come true. You can fly!" says Mama Duck and kisses him on the head.

What other animals can fly?

NAME _____

Beautiful Beginnings

1.

_____   _____   _____

2.   3.   4.

_____   _____   _____

5.   6.   7.

_____   _____   _____

Directions:
Vowels (1): Have students name each picture. Then, have them write the vowel on the line provided.
Dynamite Digraphs (2-7): Have students name each picture. Ask them to write the digraph or blend used in each word below each picture.

Spectrum Grade 1
195

Little Duck Is Scared

Little Duck stands at the edge of the pond. "I am scared, Mama Duck. What if I fall? I don't think I can fly," says Little Duck.

Will it be bad if Little Duck falls? Why or why not?

"Little Duck, don't think so much," says Mama Duck. "Just count one, two, three. Then, spread your wings and flap them up and down. Soon, you will be flying."

Do you think Little Duck can fly? How come?

Little Duck counts, "One, two, three." He flaps his wings and stops. "I just can't do this. I am not like the other ducks."

Do you think Little Duck is right? How come?

"Come on, Little Duck," says Matilda. "We can try together." Matilda flaps her wings. "One, two, three!" Matilda is flying. Little Duck watches from the ground.

Spectrum Grade 1

Go Short or Go Long: Aa

1. ate _____
2. at _____
3. ape _____
4. act _____
5. ant _____
6. age _____
7. rake _____
8. ray _____
9. able _____
10. rat _____
11. rack _____
12. rate _____
13. Andy _____
14. Alex _____
15. Abe _____

Directions:
Vowels (1–15): Have students say each word aloud. Then, have them write **short** or **long** next to the word to tell if it contains a short or a long a sound.

Spectrum Grade 1
197

Little Duck Tries

Little Duck looks up at Matilda. She is flying in the sky. "Come on, Little Duck. I know you can do it!" she calls.

Do you think Little Duck can fly? How do you know?

"Just try, Little Duck," says Mama Duck. "Count one, two, three, and flap your wings. I know you can do it, too."

Are you ever afraid to try something new? How do you think Little Duck is feeling? Why?

Little Duck looks at his mom. Next, he looks at Matilda flying in the sky. "Okay. I will try," says Little Duck.

How are Mama Duck and Matilda helping Little Duck?

Little Duck starts to flap his wings. "One," he says, and lifts his wings. "Two," he says, and lifts them again. "Threeeeeee!" Little Duck flies!

How do you think Little Duck feels about himself? How do you know?

Go Short or Go Long: Ee

1. pen _____
2. pencil _____
3. plea _____
4. pea _____
5. glee _____
6. green _____
7. tea _____
8. ten _____
9. teen _____
10. hen _____
11. fence _____
12. bee _____
13. be _____
14. bend _____
15. Ben _____

Directions:
Vowels (1-15): Have students say each word aloud. Then, ask them to write **short** or **long** next to the word to tell if it contains a short or a long e sound.

Little Duck and Matilda Fly

Little Duck and Matilda are flying. "Wow! This is fun!" says Little Duck.

"I knew you would like it," says Matilda.

Do you think flying would be fun? Why or why not?

Little Duck flaps his wings harder. He moves higher in the sky. Next, he glides through the air. Little Duck moves his wings slower. Now, he moves closer to the ground.

Have you ever watched ducks fly? What was it like?

"Wow! I think I get it! I think I know how to fly," says Little Duck.

"You are doing great!" says Matilda. "Just watch out for clouds."

"Why?" asks Little Duck.

Why should Little Duck watch out for clouds?

Little Duck turns to look at Matilda. He does not see the cloud ahead. "Little Duck! Watch out!" calls Matilda. Little Duck flies right into a giant cloud.

What do you think will happen next?

Go Short or Go Long: Ii

1. pie _____
2. pin _____
3. pine _____
4. pink _____
5. pit _____
6. tin _____
7. time _____
8. tiny _____
9. tick _____
10. Tim _____
11. die _____
12. dim _____
13. diet _____
14. dine _____
15. dinner _____

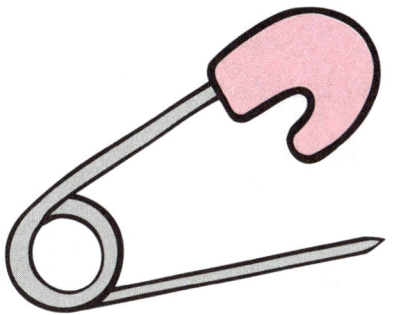

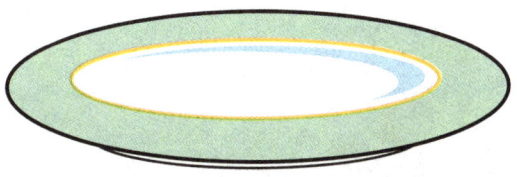

Directions:
Vowels (1-15): Have students say each word aloud. Then, ask them to write **short** or **long** next to the word to tell if it contains a short or a long i sound.

Spectrum Grade 1
201

A Cloud

Little Duck flies into a cloud. He can't see anything. Everything is white and hazy. The air gets bumpy, too. "Oh, no!" calls Little Duck.

What is happening?

Little Duck starts to fall. He tumbles around and around. Little Duck is falling out of the cloud. He is falling through the sky. He is falling toward the hard ground.

What should Little Duck do?

"Little Duck, flap your wings! Flap your wings hard," calls Matilda. Little Duck is so dizzy. He keeps falling and falling. Little Duck is close to the ground.

Why is Little Duck so dizzy?

"Little Duck, you must flap your wings!" calls Mama Duck. Little Duck sucks in air. He flaps one wing. He flaps the other. "Flap harder, Little Duck! Flap harder!" Little Duck flaps his wings as fast as he can.

What will happen to Little Duck?

Go Short or Go Long: Oo

1. pot _____
2. spot _____
3. snow _____
4. not _____
5. oat _____
6. on _____
7. box _____
8. mop _____
9. rope _____
10. Oliver _____
11. show _____
12. shop _____
13. store _____
14. stop _____
15. slope _____

Directions:
Vowels (1-15): Have students say each word aloud. Then, ask them to write **short** or **long** next to the word to tell if it contains a short or a long o sound.

Spectrum Grade 1
203

Little Duck Soars

Little Duck flaps his wings as hard as he can. He shoots up in the air again! "Good job, Little Duck! Good job!" calls Mama Duck from the ground.

How do you think Mama Duck feels? How do you know?

Little Duck flaps his wings. Little Duck shakes his head. He calls to Mama Duck below, "It's okay, Mama Duck! It's okay!"

Matilda flies next to him. "Oh my, Little Duck! You scared me. Are you all right?" she asks.

Little Duck smiles. "Yup. I'll try never to fly into a cloud again. But I can really fly, Matilda! I can do it!"

How is Little Duck feeling?

Little Duck is so happy. He flaps his wings hard. He shoots higher and higher in the sky. "Yea!" he shouts. "Honk, honk!" he calls. Matilda and Mama Duck watch him soar.

What has changed about Little Duck?

Go Short or Go Long: Uu

1. under _____
2. cube _____
3. umbrella _____
4. cut _____
5. cute _____
6. butter _____
7. yummy _____
8. mule _____
9. club _____
10. duck _____
11. dune _____
12. tuck _____
13. tune _____
14. run _____
15. funny _____

Directions:
Vowels (1–15): Have students say each word aloud. Then, ask them to write **short** or **long** next to the word to tell if it contains a short or a long u sound.

Spectrum Grade 1

Big Time Rhyme

1. funny

2. honey

3. duck

4. stop

5. ton

6. snow

7. bear

8. spring

9. fall

10. tell

11. tear

Directions:
Rhyme Time (1-11): Have students draw lines connecting the words to the pictures that rhyme.

Classified Information

1. sad   glad   mad   cage
2. five   alive   nine   thirteen
3. boat   don't   won't   did
4. wheat   seat   beat   cat
5. pie   pine   pin   spine
6. jump   true   cube   June
7. oat   coat   spot   moat
8. glee   green   gem   greet
9. hen   ten   tent   teen
10. ray   rat   rake   rate

Directions:
Grouping Together (1-10): Have students read all four words in each line. Then, tell them to circle the three words that share the same vowel sound.

Spectrum Grade 1

Carolyn Dreams of a Pet

Carolyn looked around her room. There were animals everywhere. She had teddy bears from her grandma. She had stuffed animals from her aunt. She even had posters of puppies on the wall. But what Carolyn wanted was a real pet. She wanted a kitten or a puppy to love and play with.

What do you dream of? Do you have a pet? Would you want one?

Reading Skills

1. This story is about

   _____ Carolyn wanting a pet.

   _____ Carolyn wanting a toy.

   _____ how Carolyn is sad.

2. Carolyn has posters on the walls of

   _____ horses.   _____ puppies.   _____ flowers.

3. The **setting** is where a story takes place. What is the setting for this story?

   _____ Carolyn's kitchen

   _____ Carolyn's living room

   _____ Carolyn's bedroom

4. In the picture on page 208, how does Carolyn look?

   _____ sad   _____ happy   _____ bored

Thinking Further and Predicting Outcomes

1. Do you think Carolyn will get a real pet or more teddy bears? How come?

Directions:
Reading Skills Finding the main idea (1): Have students read the question and mark the correct answer. Story Details or Cause and Effect (2-4): Have students read the question and mark the correct answer.
Thinking Further and Predicting Outcomes (1): Have students read each question, and then on a separate piece of paper write down and/or discuss their thoughts, opinions, and predictions. As the stories progress, have students discuss whether their predictions were accurate.

Spectrum Grade 1

Carolyn Talks to Her Mom

Carolyn's mom was reading a book in the den. "Mom, can I ask you something?" asked Carolyn.

"Sure, honey," said Mrs. Jones.

"Mom, I know I have teddy bears from Grandma. I even have stuffed animals from Aunt Linda. But I really want a pet I can hold and take care of," said Carolyn.

Carolyn's mom put down her book. "Pets take a lot of work," said Mrs. Jones. "And you don't just take care of a pet for a day, or a week, or even a month. Pets are part of the family for years. Do you think you would have time to take care of a pet? Why don't you really think about it."

Do you have a pet? Do you think pets are hard to take care of?

Reading Skills

1. This story is about

    _____ Carolyn hearing about how pets are bad.

    _____ Carolyn hearing about how pets take work.

    _____ Carolyn hearing about how dirty pets are.

2. Carolyn's aunt's name is _____ Lucinda. _____ Lucy. _____ Linda.

3. What does Mrs. Jones want Carolyn to do?

    _____ get a new stuffed animal

    _____ think about whether she is ready for a pet

    _____ forget about getting a pet

4. Carolyn comes to talk to Mom while Mom is

    _____ reading.   _____ working.   _____ napping.

Thinking Further and Predicting Outcomes

1. Do you think Carolyn would take good care of a pet? How come?

2. Do you think Carolyn's mother will help her get a pet? How come?

Directions:
Reading Skills Finding the main idea **(1):** Have students read the question and mark the correct answer. Story Details or Cause and Effect **(2-4):** Have students read the question and mark the correct answer.
Thinking Further and Predicting Outcomes (1-2): Have students read each question, and then on a separate piece of paper write down and/or discuss their thoughts, opinions, and predictions. As the stories progress, have students discuss whether their predictions were accurate.

Spectrum Grade 1

Time for a Pet

Carolyn went back to her room. She had just started school. Her new teacher gave her lots of homework. She had books to read and stories to write. Her class was even going to put on a school play.

Maybe she didn't have time to take care of a pet after all. Carolyn held her teddy bear tight. "What do you think I should do, teddy bear?" she asked. But the teddy bear didn't say anything at all because he wasn't real.

Do you think Carolyn has time to take care of a pet? Why or why not?

NAME _____

Reading Skills

1. In this story,

   _____ Carolyn thinks that she will have lots of time to care for a pet.

   _____ Carolyn thinks she might not have enough time for a pet.

   _____ Carolyn decides she doesn't want a pet.

2. Carolyn talks to her

   _____ aunt.   _____ teddy bear.   _____ posters.

3. In this story, Carolyn feels

   _____ excited.   _____ worried.   _____ mad.

4. Which of these is NOT something that takes up Carolyn's time?

   _____ soccer practice   _____ homework   _____ a school play

Thinking Further and Predicting Outcomes

1. Do you think Carolyn can handle both a pet and school work?

2. Do you think if Carolyn gets a pet, she will take good care of it?

3. If Carolyn had a pet, do you think she would talk to it? Why or why not?

Directions:
Reading Skills Finding the main idea (1): Have students read the question and mark the correct answer. Story Details or Cause and Effect (2-4): Have students read the question and mark the correct answer.
Thinking Further and Predicting Outcomes (1-3): Have students read each question, and then on a separate piece of paper write down and/or discuss their thoughts, opinions, and predictions. As the stories progress, have students discuss whether their predictions were accurate.

Spectrum Grade 1
213

Knock, Knock

"Knock, knock," said Carolyn's dad. He stood in the doorway. "Hi, Carolyn. Mom said you wanted a pet. What kind of pet did you want?"

"Hi, Dad. I want a pet that is soft, like a kitten or a puppy," said Carolyn.

"Well, pets like dogs and cats are a lot of work," said Mr. Jones. "How about a pet turtle or a fish tank with lots of pretty fish? We could get a blue fish or maybe even an orange and white clown fish. What do you say?"

But Carolyn was sad. She knew she could never hug a turtle or a fish.

What is your favorite animal? Do some animals make better pets than others?

NAME _____

Reading Skills

1. In this story,

_____ Carolyn's dad tells her she can't have a pet.

_____ Carolyn's dad talks about other types of pets.

_____ Carolyn's dad says he will get her a dog.

2. Carolyn's dad mentions a possible pet. It is a

_____ turtle.   _____ bunny.   _____ pony.

3. Who is the main character in the story?

_____ Mrs. Jones

_____ Mr. Jones

_____ Carolyn

4. Carolyn's mom and dad _____ about pets being a lot of work.

_____ agree   _____ do not agree

Thinking Further and Predicting Outcomes

1. Do you think Carolyn would enjoy a pet turtle?

2. Do you think Carolyn's dad knows why she wants a pet? Why or why not?

Directions:
Reading Skills Finding the main idea **(1):** Have students read the question and mark the correct answer. Story Details or Cause and Effect **(2-4):** Have students read the question and mark the correct answer.
Thinking Further and Predicting Outcomes (1-2): Have students read each question, and then on a separate piece of paper write down and/or discuss their thoughts, opinions, and predictions. As the stories progress, have students discuss whether their predictions were accurate.

Spectrum Grade 1

I Promise

Carolyn sat down for breakfast with her mom and dad. She filled her bowl with cereal. "Mom and Dad," said Carolyn, "I know I can take care of a pet. I will help feed it every morning. I will fill its bowl with water. I promise, I will always take care of it. We can name our pet 'Promise.'"

Carolyn's mom and dad looked at each other. Carolyn's mom said, "Wow, you make a good case for a pet. Dad and I will have a long talk. We will tell you our answer tomorrow."

What do you think Carolyn's parents will say? Explain your answer.

NAME _____

Reading Skills

1. In this story,

    _____ Carolyn explains how she would take care of her new pet.

    _____ Carolyn says she is sad.

    _____ Carolyn talks about her friends at school.

2. The pet will be named _____ Prince. _____ Promise. _____ Misty.

3. This story takes place

    _____ in the morning. _____ at lunchtime. _____ before bed.

4. When will Carolyn's parents tell her their answer?

    _____ tomorrow   _____ Monday   _____ after lunch

5. Who is telling the story?

    _____ Carolyn   _____ the author   _____ Carolyn's mom

Thinking Further and Predicting Outcomes

1. Do you think Carolyn has explained herself well? How do you know?

2. Do you think Carolyn's parents like her plan? Why or why not?

Directions:
Reading Skills Finding the main idea (1): Have students read the question and mark the correct answer. Story Details or Cause and Effect (2-5): Have students read the question and mark the correct answer.
Thinking Further and Predicting Outcomes (1-2): Have students read each question, and then on a separate piece of paper write down and/or discuss their thoughts, opinions, and predictions. As the stories progress, have students discuss whether their predictions were accurate.

Spectrum Grade 1

Yes or No?

All night, Carolyn tossed in her bed. She knew she could take care of a pet. She hoped her parents would say yes. She would give her pet fresh water. She would brush its fur. And she would always love it.

Carolyn's last name was Jones. So her new pet would be named "Promise Jones." She liked the name already.

Carolyn ran down the stairs at 7:00 in the morning. "Wow, you are up early!" said Carolyn's mom.

"Can we get Promise?" asked Carolyn.

"Let's call your dad in the kitchen and see," said Carolyn's mom.

Why do you think Carolyn tossed in her bed all night? Why did she get up so early?

NAME _____

Reading Skills

1. This story is about

    _____ Carolyn waking up early to find out if she will get a pet.

    _____ Carolyn waking up early to go to school.

    _____ Carolyn sleeping because she is so tired.

2. Carolyn's last name is _____ Jones. _____ Promise. _____ Linda.

3. Which of these is NOT something Carolyn will do for her pet?

    _____ brush its fur

    _____ love it

    _____ clip its nails

4. Look at the picture on page 218. Carolyn looks

    _____ excited.   _____ sneaky.   _____ grumpy.

Thinking Further and Predicting Outcomes

1. What will the decision be?

2. Why do people love pets?

3. How do you think Carolyn feels as she comes running down the stairs?

Directions:
Reading Skills Finding the main idea **(1):** Have students read the question and mark the correct answer. Story Details or Cause and Effect **(2-4):** Have students read the question and mark the correct answer.
Thinking Further and Predicting Outcomes (1-3): Have students read each question, and then on a separate piece of paper write down and/or discuss their thoughts, opinions, and predictions. As the stories progress, have students discuss whether their predictions were accurate.

Spectrum Grade 1
219

A Real Pet

Carolyn's dad walked into the kitchen. He had a big smile on his face. Carolyn was jumping in her seat. Her dad smiled like that when he said something good.

"Carolyn, your mom and I have talked all night about a pet," said her dad. "Now, if you promise to take good care of a pet, we will get one."

Carolyn ran to her dad and hugged him. Carolyn's mom joined the hug. The Jones family would soon have a real pet.

Why do you think Carolyn's parents said yes? Do you think Carolyn will keep her promise?

NAME _____

Reading Skills

1. This story is about

   _____ Carolyn finding out that she will get a pet.

   _____ Carolyn finding out that she will not get a pet.

   _____ Carolyn finding out she's late for school.

2. Carolyn hugged her _____ mother. _____ father. _____ parents.

3. Carolyn's dad has a big smile on his face when he has something _____ to say.

   _____ strange   _____ good   _____ bad

4. What is the setting for this story?

   _____ the kitchen

   _____ the den

   _____ Carolyn's bedroom

Thinking Further and Predicting Outcomes

1. Where will the Jones family get their pet?

2. Do you think Carolyn's parents made the right decision? How come?

Directions:
Reading Skills Finding the main idea (1): Have students read the question and mark the correct answer. Story Details or Cause and Effect (2-4): Have students read the question and mark the correct answer.
Thinking Further and Predicting Outcomes (1-2): Have students read each question, and then on a separate piece of paper write down and/or discuss their thoughts, opinions, and predictions. As the stories progress, have students discuss whether their predictions were accurate.

Spectrum Grade 1

Today a Pet

"Carolyn, after school we will go to the pound. There, we will look for a pet that needs a home," said Mrs. Jones.

Carolyn was so excited in school. "I'm going to get a pet today!" Carolyn told her friends.

"What kind of pet are you going to get?" asked her friend Freddy. "Will you get an alligator?"

"Nope," said Carolyn.

"Will you get a goldfish?" asked Freddy.

"Nope," said Carolyn.

"I hope to get a kitten or a puppy," said Carolyn.

Would an alligator make a good pet? Would a goldfish make a good pet? Why or why not?

NAME _____

Reading Skills

1. This story is about

_____ Carolyn telling her friends about getting a pet.

_____ Carolyn telling her friends about her school project.

_____ Carolyn's visit to the pound.

2. What was the name of Carolyn's friend who asked about her new pet? His name is

_____ Freddy.   _____ Eddie.   _____ Betty.

3. Carolyn tells Freddy that she would like to get a puppy or

_____ an alligator.

_____ a kitten.

_____ a goldfish.

4. Where will the Jones family go to get a pet?

_____ the pound   _____ the pet store   _____ a farm

Thinking Further and Predicting Outcomes

1. Do you think Carolyn will show her pet to her classmates? Why or why not?

Directions:
Reading Skills Finding the main idea **(1):** Have students read the question and mark the correct answer. Story Details or Cause and Effect **(2-4):** Have students read the question and mark the correct answer.
Thinking Further and Predicting Outcomes (1): Have students read each question, and then on a separate piece of paper write down and/or discuss their thoughts, opinions, and predictions. As the stories progress, have students discuss whether their predictions were accurate.

Spectrum Grade 1
223

Two Good Things

"Mom, why are we going to the pound? Shouldn't we go to the pet store?" said Carolyn.

"The pound is an animal shelter. It is a place where lost or unwanted animals are brought," said Mrs. Jones. "These animals really need homes. If we can find an animal here, two good things happen. We get a family pet, and an animal gets a home. The pound has all types of animals. We will see cats, dogs, and even some rabbits."

What would you do if you found a lost animal? Who would you tell?

Reading Skills

1. This story is about

_____ Carolyn learning about the pound.

_____ Carolyn wanting to go to the pet store.

_____ Carolyn changing her mind about getting a pet.

2. Mrs. Jones and Carolyn will go to the

_____ pound.   _____ pet store.   _____ zoo.

3. In the picture above, what is Carolyn thinking about?

_____ a stuffed dog   _____ a teddy bear   _____ a real dog

4. Which kind of animal will Carolyn and her mom NOT see at the pound?

_____ cats   _____ rabbits   _____ chickens

Thinking Further and Predicting Outcomes

1. Do you think it's a good idea to go to the pound for a pet? Why or why not?

2. What will Carolyn do when she chooses her pet?

Directions:
Reading Skills Finding the main idea (1): Have students read the question and mark the correct answer. Story Details or Cause and Effect (2-4): Have students read the question and mark the correct answer.
Thinking Further and Predicting Outcomes (1-2): Have students read each question, and then on a separate piece of paper write down and/or discuss their thoughts, opinions, and predictions. As the stories progress, have students discuss whether their predictions were accurate.

The Pound

Carolyn and her mom walked into a large room filled with rows of cages. Behind the bars were animals of all shapes and sizes. There were fat dogs, skinny dogs like hot dogs, furry dogs, and cages of cats. Carolyn reached her hand through the bars. She petted a sleeping kitten. Its tummy was moving up and down. Next, a fat cat licked Carolyn's hand. Its tongue felt scratchy on her hand.

What animal do you think Carolyn will pick? Why?

NAME _____

Reading Skills

1. This story is about

   _____ Carolyn seeing all sorts of animals at the pound.

   _____ Carolyn feeling scared.

   _____ Carolyn playing with a lizard.

2. Carolyn plays with a kitten that is

   _____ eating.   _____ sleeping.   _____ drinking.

3. How did the fat cat's tongue feel on Carolyn's hand?

   _____ scratchy   _____ soft   _____ slimy

4. There was only one kind of animal at the pound.

   _____ true

   _____ false

Thinking Further and Predicting Outcomes

1. Will Carolyn choose a pet after all? How do you know?

2. Will Carolyn get more than one pet? How do you know?

3. What kinds of words are used to describe the dogs?

Directions:
Reading Skills Finding the main idea (1): Have students read the question and mark the correct answer. Story Details or Cause and Effect (2-4): Have students read the question and mark the correct answer.
Thinking Further and Predicting Outcomes (1-3): Have students read each question, and then on a separate piece of paper write down and/or discuss their thoughts, opinions, and predictions. As the stories progress, have students discuss whether their predictions were accurate.

Spectrum Grade 1

Carolyn Is Sad

"Mom, who feeds all these animals?"

"The workers here feed them, but there are not enough people to brush them, or even love them."

"Mom, this makes me sad," said Carolyn.

"I know, Carolyn, but we can only take one pet. And saving one animal is a good thing," said Mrs. Jones.

"Yes," said Carolyn, and she kept looking at all the cages.

Why does Carolyn feel sad? What does Mrs. Jones say that makes Carolyn feel better?

Reading Skills

1. This story is about

   _____ Carolyn realizing that taking care of only one pet is still a good thing.

   _____ Carolyn realizing that she should take five pets.

   _____ Carolyn leaving the pound with no pets.

2. The pets are living in _____ cages. _____ houses. _____ boxes.

3. The pound needs more

   _____ cats.   _____ dogs.   _____ workers.

4. Carolyn wishes that all the animals had someone to _____ them.

   _____ wash   _____ love   _____ name

Thinking Further and Predicting Outcomes

1. Do you think Carolyn will feel better about taking only one pet? How come?

2. Do you think Carolyn is a caring person? Why or why not?

3. The next time Carolyn gets a pet, do you think she will go to the pound again? Why or why not?

Directions:
Reading Skills Finding the main idea (1): Have students read the question and mark the correct answer. Story Details or Cause and Effect (2-4): Have students read the question and mark the correct answer.
Thinking Further and Predicting Outcomes (1-3): Have students read each question, and then on a separate piece of paper write down and/or discuss their thoughts, opinions, and predictions. As the stories progress, have students discuss whether their predictions were accurate.

Spectrum Grade 1
229

Promise Jones

Carolyn did not know what to do. So many animals needed a home, and she could take only one. Carolyn went back to the sleeping kitten. It looked like a baby cloud. It was a tiny ball of soft fur. She reached her hand in the cage and petted it slowly. "I think I will take you," she said. "Your name will be Promise Jones." Just then, the kitten looked up at Carolyn.

Why do you think Carolyn chooses the kitten? What animal would you have picked? Do you think Carolyn picked a good name for her new pet? Why or why not?

NAME _____

Reading Skills

1. This story is about

   _____ Carolyn choosing a kitten.

   _____ Carolyn choosing a puppy.

   _____ Carolyn choosing two puppies.

2. What color is the kitten? _____ white _____ black _____ brown

3. Which sentence is true?

   _____ Mom had to choose for Carolyn.

   _____ Carolyn chose the sleeping kitten.

   _____ Carolyn decided to get a kitten and a puppy.

4. Carolyn thinks the kitten looks like

   _____ a baby cloud. _____ a snowball. _____ a cotton ball.

Thinking Further and Predicting Outcomes

1. Do you think Carolyn will always take good care of her kitten? How come?

2. Do you think Carolyn will be happy with her new pet? Why or why not?

Directions:
Reading Skills Finding the main idea (1): Have students read the question and mark the correct answer. Story Details or Cause and Effect (2-4): Have students read the question and mark the correct answer.
Thinking Further and Predicting Outcomes (1-2): Have students read each question, and then on a separate piece of paper write down and/or discuss their thoughts, opinions, and predictions. As the stories progress, have students discuss whether their predictions were accurate.

Spectrum Grade 1

A New Kitten

"Mom, I think this is our new pet," said Carolyn.

Carolyn's mom bent down and looked into the kitten's cage.

"Yes, she is a beautiful little kitten. I think she will like being part of our family. Let's tell the man at the desk that we have found our new pet," said Mrs. Jones.

The man behind the desk said, "New kittens need shots before they can go home with you. You can pick up your boy kitten tomorrow. He will need cat food, water, and a soft place to sleep."

Why do pets need shots? What else might a new kitten like to have?

NAME _____

Reading Skills

1. In this story,

    _____ Carolyn realizes she cannot have her kitten until tomorrow.

    _____ Carolyn learns that the kitten belongs to someone.

    _____ Carolyn learns that the kitten is 3 years old.

2. The kitten is a _____ boy. _____ girl.

3. Before the kitten can come home with Carolyn, it needs to have its _____.

    _____ food   _____ shots   _____ training

4. Mrs. Jones thinks that the kitten is

    _____ too little.   _____ too wild.   _____ beautiful.

Thinking Further and Predicting Outcomes

1. Do you think Carolyn will be upset that she can't have the kitten right away? How come?

2. Do you think Carolyn will be nervous for the kitten because he needs shots? How come?

Directions:
Reading Skills Finding the main idea (1): Have students read the question and mark the correct answer. Story Details or Cause and Effect (2-4): Have students read the question and mark the correct answer.
Thinking Further and Predicting Outcomes (1-2): Have students read each question, and then on a separate piece of paper write down and/or discuss their thoughts, opinions, and predictions. As the stories progress, have students discuss whether their predictions were accurate.

A Gift

Carolyn's dad was waiting at the front door of the house. He had a gift in his hand. Carolyn ran to her dad. "Dad, our new kitten comes tomorrow! He is so soft! He looks just like a cotton ball or a cloud," said Carolyn.

"Should we still call him Promise? If he is so soft, maybe we should call him Cloudy or Mr. Cotton," said Carolyn's dad.

"No. I already told him his name was Promise Jones," said Carolyn.

"Well, I bought food, litter, a litter box, and a gift for Promise Jones," said Carolyn's dad.

Carolyn unwrapped the gift. It was a soft cat bed shaped in a circle. A kitten would feel safe and warm inside it. Carolyn hugged her dad. "Promise Jones will love his new bed," she said.

What is the most important thing a new pet would need?

NAME _____

Reading Skills

1. This story is about

    _____ Carolyn getting a gift from her dad.

    _____ Carolyn learning to study.

    _____ Carolyn playing with Promise.

2. The new kitten is like a

    _____ cotton ball.   _____ paper.   _____ snow.

3. Carolyn's dad asks if they should call the kitten Cloudy or

    _____ Buttons.   _____ Snowy.   _____ Mr. Cotton.

4. What does Mr. Jones buy as a gift for Promise Jones?

    _____ a cat bed   _____ a scratching post   _____ litter

Thinking Further and Predicting Outcomes

1. Do you think Carolyn makes the right decision about keeping Promise's name the same? Why?

2. Do you like soft things? Why?

3. If you got a kitten, what would you name it?

Directions:
Reading Skills Finding the main idea (1): Have students read the question and mark the correct answer. Story Details or Cause and Effect (2-4): Have students read the question and mark the correct answer.
Thinking Further and Predicting Outcomes (1-3): Have students read each question, and then on a separate piece of paper write down and/or discuss their thoughts, opinions, and predictions. As the stories progress, have students discuss whether their predictions were accurate.

Spectrum Grade 1
235

Promise Jones Comes Home

The next day, Promise Jones came home. Carolyn and her mom and dad sat in the family room. Slowly, they opened the kitten carrier.

First, one tiny, white foot pressed on the rug. Then, another tiny foot came out. Next came Promise Jones' head poking out of the carrier. "Hi, Promise Jones," said Carolyn. She held out her hand. Promise looked around the room.

"Meow," he said. He walked over to Carolyn. Carolyn held him in her arms. Then, she kissed his tiny head. Carolyn said, "Promise Jones, you have found a home. We promise."

Do you think Carolyn and her family will be happy with their new pet? Why or why not? Do you think Carolyn will keep her promise with her new kitten?

NAME _____

Reading Skills

1. This story is about

_____ Carolyn promising to care for her cat.

_____ Carolyn eating dinner with her cat.

_____ Carolyn having a party with her parents.

2. Carolyn plays with her new pet in the

_____ bedroom.   _____ family room.   _____ kitchen.

3. How do you think Promise Jones felt?

_____ shy   _____ sad   _____ lazy

4. What is Carolyn's promise to her new kitten?

_____ She will play with him every day.

_____ She will not get any more pets.

_____ He has found a home.

Thinking Further and Predicting Outcomes

1. Do you think Carolyn will ever want another pet? Why?

2. Would you want somebody like Carolyn as your friend? Why or why not?

Directions:
Reading Skills Finding the main idea **(1):** Have students read the question and mark the correct answer. Story Details or Cause and Effect **(2-4):** Have students read the question and mark the correct answer.
Thinking Further and Predicting Outcomes (1-2): Have students read each question, and then on a separate piece of paper write down and/or discuss their thoughts, opinions, and predictions. As the stories progress, have students discuss whether their predictions were accurate.

Spectrum Grade 1

Revisiting Blends

1.

_____   _____   _____

2.

_____   _____   _____

3. It has lots of animals.
It is fun to visit.
You can learn a lot.
What is it?

a school

a zoo

the moon

4. You can swim here.
It feels cool. Have fun!
What is it?

a pool

a bathtub

a glass of water

Directions:
Blends (1-2): Ask students to say each picture aloud and listen to the beginning sound. Have them write the beginning blend on the line below the picture.
Making Sense (3-4): Ask students to circle the answer that makes the most sense.

Finding the Correct Word

1. Do you like to _____ songs?

   sing

   sings

   sang

2. The duck enjoys _____ corn.

   eaten

   eating

   to eat

3. Jimmy has _____ into the pool.

   jumping

   jumped

   jump

4. Josefina _____ to play piano.

   like

   likes

   liking

5.

   _____   _____   _____

   _____   _____   _____

Directions:
Sentence Completion (1-4): Have students circle the word that best completes the sentence.
Sequence (5): Have the student look at all six pictures. Ask the student to write **1** below the event that would happen first, **2** below the event that would happen second, and so on.

Blends Review

1.
___ ___

2.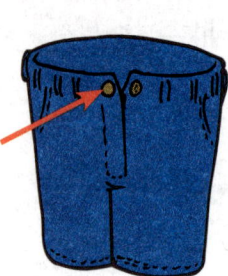
___ ___

3.
___ ___

4.
___ ___

5.
___ ___

6.
___ ___

7.
___ ___

8.
___ ___

Directions:
Blends and Ending Consonants (1-8): Have the student look at each picture and say it aloud. Ask them to listen to the beginning blends and ending consonants. Then, have him or her write down the beginning blends and ending consonants next to each word.

Spectrum Grade 1

NAME _____

Blends Review

1.

_____   _____   _____

2.

_____   _____   _____

3.

zba ___ ___ ___   hia ___ ___ ___

guk ___ ___ ___   bnu ___ ___ ___

Directions:
Beginning Consonants (1): Ask students to say each picture aloud and listen to the beginning sound. Have them write the beginning letter on the line below the picture.
Blends (2): Ask students to say each picture aloud and listen to the beginning sound. Have them write the beginning blend on the line below the picture.
Alphabetical Order (3): Ask students to put the three letters in each group in alphabetical order.

Spectrum Grade 1
241

NAME _____

Where Are You?

1.

next to   over   above   below | in   over   under   below

2.

under   inside   around   below | outside   inside   under   below

3.

in   next to   around   above | in   beneath   under   next to

4.

down   up   sideways   under | down   up   around   near

Directions:
Using the Pictures (1-4): Have the student look at the pictures. Ask him or her to circle the word that describes where the objects are located.

NAME _____

Classify Me

1. three   six   five   food
2. orange   lemon   lime   ham
3. penny   dime   nickel   dollar
4. mouse   rat   bug   lion
5. truck   car   boat   bus
6. June   July   August   flag
7. green   yellow   brown   tired
8. stone   rock   brick   rug
9. mom   dad   dog   sister
10. funny   smile   laugh   mad

Directions:
Grouping Together (1-10): Have students read all four words in each line. Ask them to circle the three words that go together.

Spectrum Grade 1

Alaska

Alaska is the largest state in America. It is the coldest state. It is two times as big as Texas and home to bears and eagles. If you lived in Alaska, you might see a blue glacier shining in the sun. Maybe you would see a bear, a moose, or even a pod of whales.

Juneau is the capital of Alaska. It is named after Joe Juneau. He went to Alaska in search of gold.

Many people in Alaska like to make and eat special ice cream. They mix berries with snow and seal oil.

NAME _____

Reading Skills

1. What might you see if you lived in Alaska?

   _____ robins

   _____ moose

   _____ lions

2. Alaska is _____ as big as Texas.
   two times   three times   ten times

3. What did Joe Juneau search for in Alaska? _____
   bears   gold   diamonds

4. Which state is bigger?

   _____ Alaska   _____ Texas

5. What is the special ice cream in Alaska made from?

   _____ berries, cream, and seal oil

   _____ snow, seal oil, and fish

   _____ berries, snow, and seal oil

Thinking Further

1. Would you want to live in Alaska? Why or why not?

2. What are a few words that describe Alaska?

Directions:
Reading Skills—Comprehension and Facts and Details (1-5): Have students read the question and mark the correct answer.
Thinking Further (1-2): Have students read each question and then discuss their responses, or have them write down their thoughts on a separate sheet of paper.

Spectrum Grade 1
245

New Mexico

New Mexico is a state full of red clay mountains. The capital of New Mexico is Santa Fe. It is the oldest capital city in America. This very old city was founded in 1610!

In Taos, New Mexico, you can see brown adobe houses. They are made from clay bricks baked in the sun.

In New Mexico, you might see bunches of red chili peppers. These are hung on strings outside houses. Sometimes, people leave the red chilies out all winter. They look beautiful in the white snow.

NAME _____

Reading Skills

1. What might you see if you lived in New Mexico?

   _____ bunches of chili peppers

   _____ bunches of bananas

   _____ bunches of green peppers

2. Santa Fe was founded in _____ 1610. _____ 1615. _____ 1910.

3. Adobe houses are made from _____ bricks.

   _____ clay   _____ rock   _____ concrete

4. Why does Santa Fe have a star next to it on the map of New Mexico?

   _____ The author lives there.

   _____ It is the biggest city.

   _____ It is the capital.

Thinking Further

1. Would you want to live in New Mexico? Why or why not?

2. What are a few words that describe New Mexico?

3. Were you surprised to find out that it snows in New Mexico? Why or why not?

Directions:
Reading Skills—Comprehension and Facts and Details (1-4): Have students read the question and mark the correct answer.
Thinking Further (1-3): Have students read each question and then discuss their responses, or have them write down their thoughts on a separate sheet of paper.

Spectrum Grade 1

Oregon

Long, long ago, many people heard secrets about Oregon. They headed where the soil was good for farming. Many people wanted to travel across America to this state. They wanted to plant crops.

Traveling across America in a covered wagon was very dangerous. Travelers could go only in summer. They had to beat the coming cold weather. Many people on the Oregon Trail did not have enough food or fresh water. Many travelers died.

Today, you can visit Oregon by car, plane, or train. Maybe you'd want to visit Crater Lake National Park and see America's deepest lake.

NAME _____

Reading Skills

1. What might you see if you visited Oregon?

   _____ the deepest lake   _____ the widest lake

   _____ the coldest lake

2. Some people went to Oregon because it had _____ soil.

   rich   poor   dirty

A **table of contents** tells you where to find things in a book. Use this table of contents to answer the questions.

Table of Contents
Map of Oregon 3
The Oregon Trail 5
Oregon's Natural Beauty 17
Famous People of Oregon 25
Oregon Today 33

3. If you want to find out about Oregon's national parks, turn to page (5, 17).

4. If you want to find out where the city of Portland, Oregon is, turn to page (3, 25).

Thinking Further

1. Do you think there are farmers in Oregon? How do you know?

2. What are a few words that describe Oregon?

Directions:
Reading Skills—Comprehension and Facts and Details (1-4): Have students read the question and mark the correct answer.
Thinking Further (1-2): Have students read each question and then discuss their responses, or have them write down their thoughts on a separate sheet of paper.

Spectrum Grade 1
249

Rhode Island

Rhode Island is the smallest state in America. It is nicknamed "Little Rhody."

If you visit, you might want to ride America's oldest merry-go-round in Watch Hill.

Maybe you'd want to take a ferry ride to Block Island. This is a tiny island off the coast. French pirates are said to have landed there. Captain Kidd's gold is thought to still be buried on the beautiful island.

NAME _____

Reading Skills

1. What island could you see in Rhode Island?

   _____ Block Island

   _____ Kidd Island

   _____ Watch Island

2. Rhode Island is the _____ state.

   smallest   largest   prettiest

3. Rhode Island has a nickname. It is

   _____ "Little Rhody."

   _____ "Bay State."

   _____ "Pirate State."

4. If you wanted to go to Block Island, you could take a

   _____ ferry.   _____ train.   _____ bus.

Thinking Further

1. Would you want to travel to Block Island? Why or why not?

2. Give Rhode Island another nickname.

3. Do you think that Captain Kidd's gold is still buried on Block Island? Why or why not?

Directions:
Reading Skills—Comprehension and Facts and Details (1-4): Have students read the question and mark the correct answer.
Thinking Further (1-3): Have students read each question and then discuss their responses, or have them write down their thoughts on a separate sheet of paper.

Spectrum Grade 1

Vermont

Vermont gets its name from two French words. *Vert* means *green*, and *mont* means *mountain*. Vermont is known as the "Green Mountain" state. If you go to Vermont, you should see a sugarhouse. A sugarhouse is where maple tree sap is turned into maple syrup. Try some on your pancakes. You can also hike up Bread Loaf Mountain. This mountain looks like a green loaf of bread!

NAME _____

Reading Skills

1. What might you see if you live in Vermont?

   _____ green mountains   _____ green rivers

   _____ blue mountains

2. You can climb

   _____ Bread Loaf Mountain.   _____ Meatloaf Mountain.

   _____ Butter Mountain.

3. Maple tree sap is turned into syrup. This happens in a

   _____ milk house.   _____ sugarhouse.   _____ sap house.

4. What does Vermont's name mean?

   _____ Tall Mountains   _____ Maple Mountains

   _____ Green Mountains

5. Vermont's name comes from two _____ words.

   _____ Spanish   _____ German   _____ French

Thinking Further

1. Would you want to live in Vermont? Why or why not?

2. What kind of tree is in the picture on page 252? How do you know?

Directions:
Reading Skills—Comprehension and Facts and Details (1-5): Have students read the question and mark the correct answer.
Thinking Further (1-2): Have students read each question and then discuss their responses, or have them write down their thoughts on a separate sheet of paper.

Spectrum Grade 1
253

New Hampshire

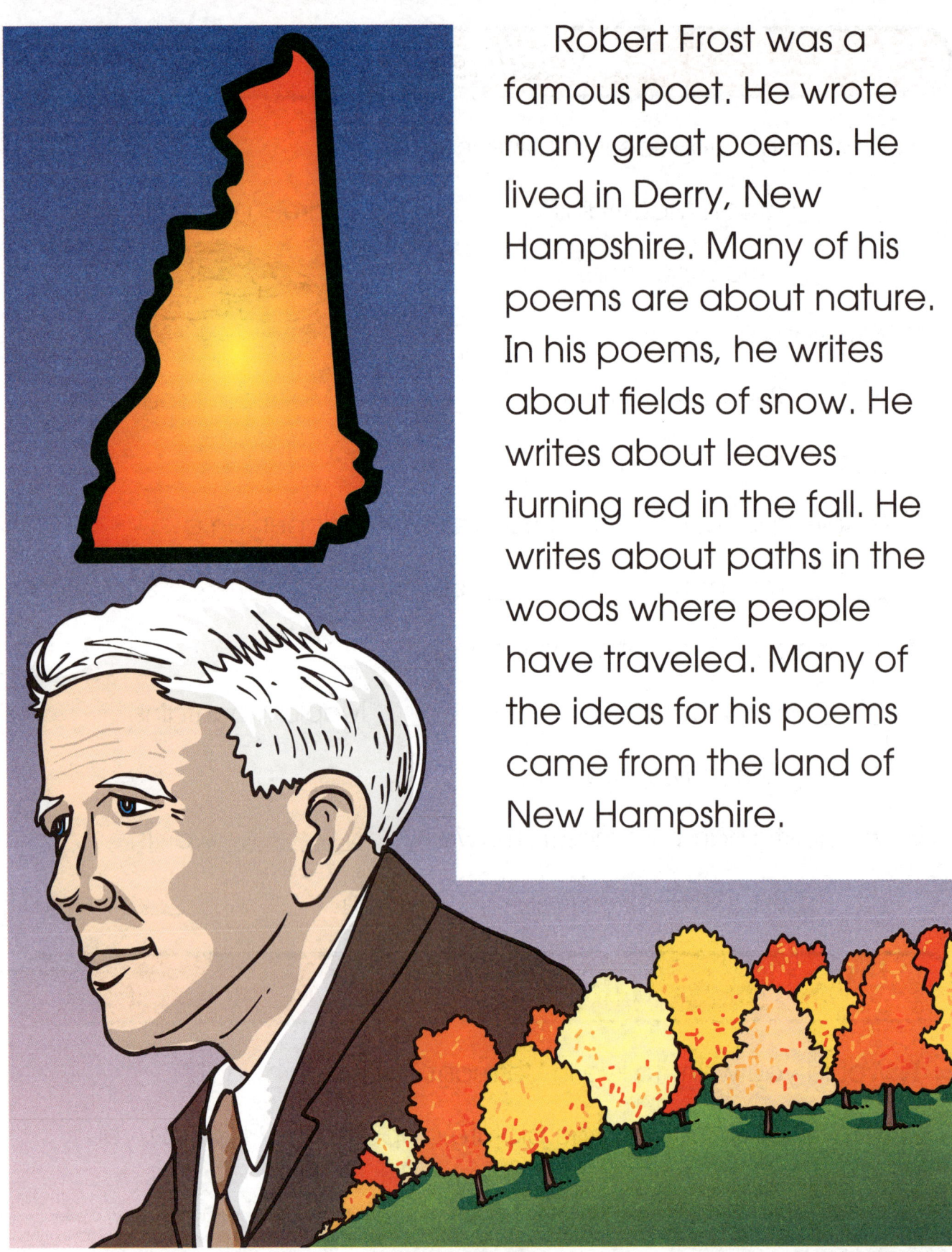

Robert Frost was a famous poet. He wrote many great poems. He lived in Derry, New Hampshire. Many of his poems are about nature. In his poems, he writes about fields of snow. He writes about leaves turning red in the fall. He writes about paths in the woods where people have traveled. Many of the ideas for his poems came from the land of New Hampshire.

Reading Skills

1. Robert Frost was a famous

   _____ songwriter.

   _____ poet.

   _____ singer.

2. Many of his poems are about

   _____ roses.   _____ buildings.   _____ nature.

3. What do you think Robert Frost would rather write a poem about?

   _____ bikes   _____ trees   _____ trucks

4. Which of these statements is NOT true?

   _____ Robert Frost lived in a town called Derry.

   _____ Robert Frost wrote poems about fall leaves.

   _____ No one knows where Robert got his ideas.

Thinking Further

1. Would you want to live in New Hampshire? Why or why not?

2. What would you like to write a poem about?

Directions:
Reading Skills—Comprehension and Facts and Details (1-4): Have students read the question and mark the correct answer.
Thinking Further (1-2): Have students read each question and then discuss their responses, or have them write down their thoughts on a separate sheet of paper.

Spectrum Grade 1

Montana

Montana is called "Big Sky Country." The big, blue sky seems to meet the land. One thing to visit here is Grasshopper Glacier. Millions of grasshoppers are frozen in the glacier ice for you to see.

Montana has more than 50 mountain ranges. Rocky Mountain goats call the rocks home. These white and furry goats can walk on sharp rocks. The goats are hard to see because they live so high up on the rocks.

NAME _____

Reading Skills

1. Montana is called

   _____ "Big Time."

   _____ "Big Sky Country."

   _____ "Big Cow."

2. Grasshopper Glacier has _____ of frozen grasshoppers.

   _____ a couple   _____ hundreds   _____ millions

3. Why are the Rocky Mountain goats hard to see?

   _____ There are only a few of them.

   _____ They blend in with the mountain.

   _____ They live high up on the rocks.

4. In Montana, the sky seems to meet the

   _____ land.   _____ sea.   _____ lake.

Thinking Further

1. Would you want to live in Montana? Why or why not?

2. Which would you want to see more, a grasshopper, glacier, or a Rocky Mountain goat? Explain why.

Directions:
Reading Skills—Comprehension and Facts and Details (1-4): Have students read the question and mark the correct answer.
Thinking Further (1-2): Have students read each question and then discuss their responses, or have them write down their thoughts on a separate sheet of paper.

Spectrum Grade 1
257

Nevada

Nevada is the driest state in the United States. It has many human-made lakes. These lakes help bring water to the land. Two places you might want to visit here are a lake and a dam.

Lake Tahoe is a beautiful lake. It has snowy mountains all around it. It also has some of the clearest water.

Hoover Dam was named after the 31st president. Huge piles of cement were used to make the dam strong. The same amount of cement could be used to build a highway from New York City all the way to San Francisco!

NAME _____

Reading Skills

1. Nevada is the _____ state in the United States.

   _____ rainiest

   _____ driest

   _____ hottest

2. Huge piles of cement were used to make Hoover Dam

   _____ strong.   _____ gray.   _____ cold.

3. Who was Hoover Dam named after?

   _____ the person who built it

   _____ a president

   _____ the governor of Nevada

4. The water in Lake Tahoe is

   _____ clear.   _____ cloudy.   _____ shallow.

Thinking Further

1. Would you want to live in Nevada? Why or why not?

2. Would you want to help build a giant water dam? Why or why not?

Directions:
Reading Skills—Comprehension and Facts and Details (1-4): Have students read the question and mark the correct answer.
Thinking Further (1-2): Have students read each question and then discuss their responses, or have them write down their thoughts on a separate sheet of paper.

Spectrum Grade 1

Hawaii

Hawaii is the 50th state. Over 100 islands make up Hawaii. New islands are still being made. These islands are made from volcanoes! Hawaii has black sand beaches also made from volcanoes.

The islands of Hawaii are in the middle of the Pacific Ocean. Some plants and animals found on Hawaii cannot be seen anywhere else.

If you visit Hawaii, you can visit a volcano. You can visit a black sand beach. When you get off the plane, people will say *aloha*. *Aloha* is how people welcome you in Hawaii. *Aloha* also means *love*.

NAME _____

Reading Skills

1. Over _____ islands make up Hawaii.

   _____ one hundred

   _____ two hundred

   _____ three hundred

2. The word *aloha* means

   _____ *like.*   _____ *pretty.*   _____ *love.*

3. Volcanoes make Hawaii's

   _____ islands.   _____ weather.   _____ oceans.

4. Saying *aloha* is a way to _____ people.

   _____ confuse

   _____ welcome

   _____ call

Thinking Further

1. Would you want to live in Hawaii? Why or why not?

2. Would you want to tour a volcano?

3. What is unusual about some of the plants and animals in Hawaii?

Directions:
Reading Skills—Comprehension and Facts and Details (1-4): Have students read the question and mark the correct answer.
Thinking Further (1-3): Have students read each question and then discuss their responses, or have them write down their thoughts on a separate sheet of paper.

Spectrum Grade 1
261

Maryland

Maryland is known as "mini America." Here, you can see bays. You can see valleys. Maryland has beaches. Maryland has mountains, too.

If you visit this state, you can take a boat ride on the bay. You can visit the harbor where Francis Scott Key wrote a famous song. He was on a boat when he wrote the national anthem for America. Maryland has things for everybody to do.

NAME _____

Reading Skills

1. What might you see in Maryland?

   _____ bays

   _____ a rain forest

   _____ the tallest mountain

2. Maryland has things to do for

   _____ everybody.   _____ a few people.

3. Which of these is Maryland's nickname?

   _____ "little America"   _____ "the Bay State"

   _____ "mini America"

4. Francis Scott Key was on a _____ in a harbor when he wrote America's anthem.

   _____ plane   _____ boat   _____ beach

Thinking Further

1. Would you like to live in Maryland? Why or why not?

2. What would you nickname Maryland?

3. How do you think Maryland got its nickname?

Directions:
Reading Skills—Comprehension and Facts and Details (1-4): Have students read the question and mark the correct answer.
Thinking Further (1-3): Have students read each question and then discuss their responses, or have them write down their thoughts on a separate sheet of paper.

Spectrum Grade 1
263

California

California is the state with the most people in it. It is the third largest state.

This is a state where you can ski on a mountain. A few hours later, you can swim in the sea! In this state, you can see redwood forests and huge deserts.

This is a state where lots of movies are made. Many computer games are created here, too. This is a fun state to visit.

NAME _____

Reading Skills

1. What might you see in California?

   _____ movie making   _____ cornfields

   _____ kangaroos

2. Why do so many people visit California?

   _____ There are many pretty places to visit.

   _____ There are lots of cars.

   _____ There are lots of people.

3. Based on the article, you know that California is near

   _____ the ocean.   _____ Florida.   _____ a big lake.

4. **California is the largest state.** Is this true or false?

   _____ true   _____ false

Thinking Further

1. Would you like to live in California? Why or why not?

2. What would you nickname California?

3. Look at the picture near the top of this page. What does it help you understand about California?

Directions:
Reading Skills—Comprehension and Facts and Details (1-4): Have students read the question and mark the correct answer.
Thinking Further (1-3): Have students read each question and then discuss their responses, or have them write down their thoughts on a separate sheet of paper.

Spectrum Grade 1

Minnesota

It is freezing cold! Winters in Minnesota can be so cold that wet hair turns to ice. Bundle up!

The summers are warm. You can go fishing or boating. You can swim in many of the state's thousands of lakes.

Minnesota is also home to two big cities. These cities are next to each other. They are Minneapolis and St. Paul. These two cities are known as the "Twin Cities."

NAME _____

Reading Skills

1. Winters in Minnesota can be so cold that wet hair turns to

   _____ snow.

   _____ ice.

   _____ dark.

2. Where might you go swimming in Minnesota?

   _____ lakes   _____ parks   _____ oceans

3. The cities of Minneapolis and St. Paul are known as the

   _____ "Double Cities."   _____ "Twin Cities."

   _____ "Chilly Cities."

4. Fishing and boating are fun to do in Minnesota during the

   _____ winter.   _____ summer.

Thinking Further

1. Would you want to visit Minnesota? Why or why not?

2. What are two words that describe Minnesota?

3. If you lived in Minnesota, would you like summer or winter better? Why?

Directions:
Reading Skills—Comprehension and Facts and Details (1-4): Have students read the question and mark the correct answer.
Thinking Further (1-3): Have students read each question and then discuss their responses, or have them write down their thoughts on a separate sheet of paper.

Spectrum Grade 1

Colorado

Denver is the capital of Colorado. It is also a mile up in the sky. It is called the "Mile High City."

Colorado is a state in the Rocky Mountains. Many people love to visit and go skiing. Some people bike the mountain paths. Other people like to ride rafts in the wild rivers there.

NAME _____

Reading Skills

1. The city of Denver is _____ in the sky.

_____ low

_____ high

_____ blue

2. Some people come to this state to

_____ ski.   _____ surf.   _____ see fish.

3. What is the capital of Colorado?

_____ Rocky Mountain

_____ Mile City

_____ Denver

Thinking Further

1. Would you like to ski, bike, or raft in Colorado? Why?

2. What are two words to describe Colorado?

3. What does the red star by Denver on the map mean?

Directions:
Reading Skills—Comprehension and Facts and Details (1-3): Have students read the question and mark the correct answer.
Thinking Further (1-3): Have students read each question and then discuss their responses, or have them write down their thoughts on a separate sheet of paper.

Spectrum Grade 1
269

Words to Know

1.  duck / dog / did

2.  for / fish / from

3.  grass / green / go

4.  bowl / bee / big

5.  call / can't / cold

6.  water / wet / won't

7. 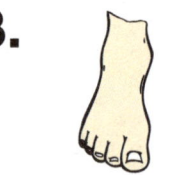 pond / put / play

8.  foot / farm / for

9.  can / class / corn

10.  hop / hat / him

11.  road / run / red

12.  sun / son / sit

13.  pull / push / pail

14. soft / set / says

15. sleep / slip / sled

Directions:
Recognizing Familiar Words (1-15): Ask students to say the name of each picture and then circle the word that best describes the picture.

Spectrum Grade 1

NAME _____

Words to Know

1.  snap / snail / snore

2.  has / hand / her

3.  pine / penny / pinch

4.  was / wing / wish

5.  fox / for / from

6.  dinner / dime / don't

7.  am / apple / ape

8.  want / wish / will

9.  whale / wink / what

10. 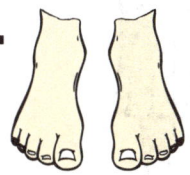 friend / feet / from

11.  fly / fry / fun

12.  sun / star / skip

13.  kit / kite / kiss

14.  gift / give / get

15.  string / step / skunk

Directions:
Recognizing Familiar Words (1-15): Ask students to say the name of each picture and then circle the word that best describes the picture.

Spectrum Grade 1

NAME _____

Contractions

1. do not _____

2. let us _____

3. will not _____

4. was not _____

5. is not _____

6. that is _____

7. can not _____

8. did not _____

9. I will _____

Directions:
Introducing Contractions (1-9): Explain the concept of contractions to students. Ask them to read aloud the contractions at the top of the page. Then, ask students to read the numbered pair of words. Next, have students write the correct contraction for the two words.

Spectrum Grade 1

Lost Letters

1. Why does Little Duck want to fly?

He wants to see the blue s___y.

2. How can he fly?

With his w___ngs.

3. Do boys and girls have wings?

N___t that I can se___.

4. Do fish have wings?

N___, but they have f___ns.

5. Can Little Duck dive?

Yes, he can d___ve.

Directions:
Missing Letters (1-5): Have students read each sentence and fill in the missing letters.

Lost Letters

1. What animal did Carolyn pick?

She picked a k____tten.

2. How did the kitten feel?

The new kitten felt s____ft.

3. What kind of pets do most people have?

Most people have c____ts or d____gs.

4. Do some people have different pets?

Max has a pet fr____g and a pet t____rtle.

5. Would a tiger make a good pet?

No, a tiger wo____'t make a good pet.

Directions:
Missing Letters (1-5): Have students read each sentence and fill in the missing letters.

Spectrum Grade 1

Words to Know

1. hall / home / hop
2. bear / bee / big
3. pat / pet / pit
4. green / great / good
5. bench / boat / belt
6. like / love / log
7. to / two / toe
8. bend / back / bath
9. big / bring / bow
10. bars / bug / birds
11. call / can't / can
12. land / lick / lip
13. can / cage / call
14. play / pan / pin
15. ran / run / rock

Directions:
Recognizing Familiar Words (1-15): Ask students to say the name of each picture and then circle the word that best describes the picture.

Spectrum Grade 1

Math Grade 1 Answers

Lesson 1.1, page 6

2	3
2	3
	3
	3
1	2
1	2
1	2
1	2
3	0
3	0
3	
3	

Lesson 1.2, page 7

1	0
1	0
2	1
2	1
2	0
2	0
0	1
0	1

Lesson 1.3, page 8

5	4
5	4
5	
5	
4	5
4	5
4	5
4	5
4	5
4	5
4	5

Lesson 1.4, page 9

6	6
6	6
6	6
6	6
6	6
6	6
6	6
6	
6	

6	6	5	6	6	5
5	6	6			
6	6	4			

Lesson 1.5, page 10

3	0
3	0
2	4
2	4
5	3
5	3
1	1
1	1

Lesson 1.6, page 11

2	5
2	5

Math Grade 1 Answers

6	3
6	3
4	1
4	1

5 3 4 0 2 1

Lesson 1.7, page 12

5 5 3 2	6 6 1 5
4	6
4	3
1	
3	
3 3 2 1	4 4 0 4
4 2	5 5 1 4

Lesson 1.8, page 13

3
4
2
3
5
5

Lesson 1.9, page 14

7	7
7	7
7	7
7	7
7	7
7	7
7	7
7	7

7 7 6 7 7 7

Lesson 1.10, page 15

4	6
4	6
2	7
2	7
1	3
1	3
5	0
5	0

Lesson 1.11, page 16

8	8
8	8
8	8
8	8
8	8
8	8
8	
8	

7 8 8 8 7 8

Lesson 1.12, page 17

6	4
6	4
2	1
2	1
7	0
7	0
5	3
5	3

Spectrum Grade 1

Math Grade 1 Answers

Lesson 1.13, page 18

9	9
9	9
9	9
9	9
9	9
9	9
9	9
9	9
9	9
9	9

9 9 9 9 9 9

Lesson 1.14, page 19

2	6
2	6
4	8
4	8
7	5
7	5

3 0 9 1

Lesson 1.15, page 20

10	10
10	10
10	10
10	10
10	10
10	10
10	10
10	10

10 10 10 10 10 10

Lesson 1.16, page 21

4	5
4	5
7	2
7	2
9	0
9	0
8	1
8	1
3	6
3	6

Lesson 1.17, page 22

9 9 5 4   10 10 7 3
   7   9
   7   9
   2   3
   5   6

8 8 7 1   10 5

7 7 3 4   8 8 6 2

Lesson 1.18, page 23

10
9
8
7
10

Math Grade 1 Answers

Lesson 1.19, page 24

7¢	10¢
8¢	9¢
10¢	5¢
8¢	6¢

Lesson 1.20, page 25

7¢
10¢
8¢
5¢
1¢
9¢

Lesson 1.21, page 26

9
9
8
8
8
6
9
10
7

Lesson 1.22, page 27

4	4
7	7
5	5
6	6
4	4
6	6
2	2
1	1
3	3

Lesson 1.23, page 28

	4	6	7
2	3		10
	6	8	9
	8		2
4	5	6	7

Lesson 2.1, page 29

1 ten 0 ones = 10
1 ten 1 one = 11
1 ten 2 ones = 12
1 ten 3 ones = 13
1 ten 4 ones = 14

Lesson 2.2, page 30

1 ten 5 ones = 15
1 ten 6 ones = 16
1 ten 7 ones = 17
1 ten 8 ones = 18
1 ten 9 ones = 19

Lesson 2.3, page 31

2 tens 0 ones = 20
2 tens 1 one = 21
2 tens 2 ones = 22
2 tens 3 ones = 23
2 tens 4 ones = 24

Math Grade 1 Answers

Lesson 2.4, page 32

2 tens 5 ones = 25
2 tens 6 ones = 26
2 tens 7 ones = 27
2 tens 8 ones = 28
2 tens 9 ones = 29

Lesson 2.5, page 33

3 tens 4 ones = 34
4 tens 2 ones = 42
3 tens 0 ones = 30
4 tens 3 ones = 43

44	39
36	45
41	37
38	40
46	33

Lesson 2.6, page 34

5 tens 1 one = 51
6 tens 3 ones = 63
5 tens 4 ones = 54
6 tens 2 ones = 62

60	69
52	64
67	55
53	66
58	57

Lesson 2.7, page 35

76	98
83	80
71	75
87	99
94	91
92	86
79	70
88	82

Lesson 2.8, page 36

1	2	3	4	5	6	7	8	9	10
11	12	13	14	15	16	17	18	19	20
21	22	23	24	25	26	27	28	29	30
31	32	33	34	35	36	37	38	39	40
41	42	43	44	45	46	47	48	49	50
51	52	53	54	55	56	57	58	59	60
61	62	63	64	65	66	67	68	69	70
71	72	73	74	75	76	77	78	79	80
81	82	83	84	85	86	87	88	89	90
91	92	93	94	95	96	97	98	99	100
101	102	103	104	105	106	107	108	109	110
111	112	113	114	115	116	117	118	119	120

Lesson 2.9, page 37

94, 97, 100, 101
66, 69, 72, 76
102, 105, 107, 110
5, 20, 40, 60
10, 40, 60, 90, 100, 110, 120
78, 75, 71, 68
83, 80, 76, 75
20, 14, 10, 4
115, 100, 85, 80
65, 50, 30, 20
110, 100, 80, 50, 40, 20

Math Grade 1 Answers

Lesson 2.10, page 38

16 < 22	78 > 38	86 < 88
37 > 18	45 = 45	15 < 26
51 < 56	73 < 99	92 = 92
70 = 70	24 < 25	19 > 11
35 < 74	40 > 30	48 < 89
81 > 43	13 = 13	36 > 34
12 < 20	33 < 42	63 = 63
62 > 41	21 > 17	71 > 61

Lesson 2.10, page 39

77 < 87	97 < 98	6 < 49
90 > 80	4 < 27	69 > 58
79 > 5	46 < 75	1 < 10
53 > 32	94 > 82	50 < 93
64 = 64	67 > 29	95 > 3
84 < 96	60 > 39	15 > 11
23 > 9	55 < 72	63 = 63
57 < 85	2 < 68	59 < 83
52 > 31	91 > 8	47 > 37
47 = 47	66 < 83	50 = 50
28 > 7	14 < 59	21 < 31
44 < 54	76 > 65	35 > 23

Lesson 3.1, page 40

11
11
11
11
11
11
11
11
11 12 11 11 10 11

Lesson 3.2, page 41

3	8
6	5
7	4
9	2

8 5 2 3 7 11

Lesson 3.3, page 42

12	12
12	12
12	12

13 12 12 12 13 12
11 12 12
12 12 12

Lesson 3.4, page 43

5	7
6	4
3	9

8 9 4 5 6 7
3 4 6
5 9 8

Lesson 3.5, page 44

13	13
13	13
13	13

13 13 13 12 13 13

Spectrum Grade 1

Math Grade 1 Answers

13	13	12
13	11	13

Lesson 3.6, page 45

4	9
7	13
5	8

4 5 8 6 13 7
6 5 9
8 4 7

Lesson 3.7, page 46

14	14
14	14
14	14

13 15 14 14 14 14
13 14 14

Lesson 3.8, page 47

8 6
9 5
7 14

14 7 6 5 8 9
7 5 8
6 12 11

Lesson 3.9, page 48

14 14 11 3
15 15 0 15

13	13	12	1
15	15	12	3

Lesson 3.10, page 49

15 15
15 14 15 13 14 13
15 13 15 14 14 13
6 9
6 7 9 5 8 6
8 9 9 4 7 6

Lesson 3.11, page 50

17 17 14 3
18 18 16 2
19 19 18 1
20 20 4 16

Lesson 3.12, page 51

16 16
14 16 15 16 14 15
15 14 16 14 14 15
7 9
8 8 5 6 7 9
9 6 7 9 7 8

Lesson 3.13, page 52

14,14; 15,15; 14, 14; 17, 17; 11, 11; 12, 12; 15, 15; 14, 14; 13, 13

Math Grade 1 Answers

Lesson 3.14, page 53

17 18
16 17 14 15 18 14
15 14 17 15 16 15
8 9 9
7 8 7 9 9 9
9 8 7 8 8 9

Lesson 3.15, page 54

8
18
17
9
9

Lesson 3.16, page 55

13, 13; 13, 13; 12, 12; 11, 11; 12, 12; 11, 11; 12, 12;
11, 11; 12, 12

Lesson 3.17, page 56

12; 19; 10; 10; 17; 15; 18; 17; 16

Lesson 4.1, page 57

17 25 32 26 17
46 28 32 49 15
68 59 89 45 88

Lesson 4.2, page 58

25 39 43 41 67
43 69 57 61 90
85 90 95 92 92
38 92 60 79 85

57 31 79 96 95

Lesson 4.3, page 59

40 20
10 10
10 20

Lesson 4.4, page 60

17 16 25 35 33 44
58 76 65 27 84 100
93 34 85 16 54 73
10 10 20 10 50 20
10 40 0 30 50 30
0 10 60 20 10 60

Lesson 4.5, page 61

18 19 9 20 6
7 11 17 8 6
10 17 16 19 20

Lesson 5.1, page 62

4:00	9:00
four o'clock	nine o'clock
3:00	7:00
three o'clock	seven o'clock
12:00	2:00
twelve o'clock	two o'clock
1:00	6:00
one o'clock	six o'clock

Math Grade 1 Answers

Lesson 5.1, page 63

6:00	7:00
8:00	2:00
🕗	🕑
🕕	🕖

Lesson 5.2, page 64

1:30 one thirty	5:30 five thirty
7:30 seven thirty	10:30 ten thirty
12:30 twelve thirty	2:30 two thirty
6:30 six thirty	9:30 nine thirty

Lesson 5.2, page 65

4:30	11:30
8:30	3:30
🕟	🕦
🕣	🕞

Lesson 5.3, page 66

3 1 2	3 2 1
2 3 1	3 1 2
2	3 1 2
3	
1	

Lesson 5.4, page 67

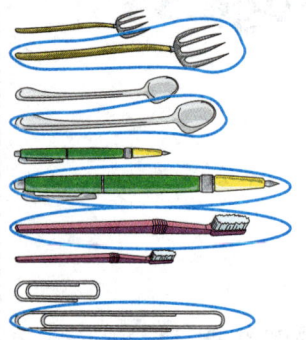

Lesson 5.5, page 68

7	8
4	5
6	
5	

Math Grade 1 Answers

Lesson 5.6, page 69

6
8
4
7
10

Lesson 5.7, page 70

less than
greater than
equal to
greater than

Lesson 5.8, page 71

Answers will vary.

Lesson 5.8, page 72

Answers will vary.

Lesson 6.1, page 73

S	T	T	C
C	R	T	R
R	S	S	C
T	C	C	S
R	T	S	R

Lesson 6.2, page 74

□
△
□

Lesson 6.3, page 75

Triangle △
Square □
Rectangle
Triangle △
Circle ○

Lesson 6.4, page 76

○   ⬠
⬡   ○

Spectrum Grade 1
285

Math Grade 1 Answers

Lesson 6.5, page 77

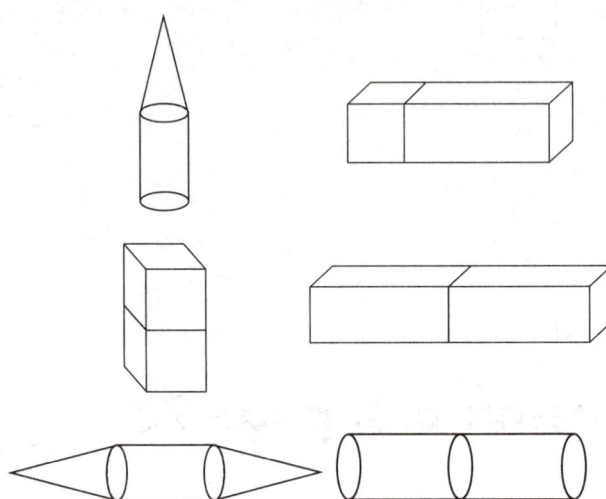

Lesson 6.6, page 78

Answers will vary but the apple and soap should be divided in half. Answers will vary but the rug and orange should be divided in thirds. Answers will vary but the peach and coloring page should be divided in fourths.

Lesson 6.7, page 79

4, 1, $\frac{1}{4}$; 2, 1, $\frac{1}{2}$
2, 1, $\frac{1}{2}$; 4, 1, $\frac{1}{4}$
one-half; one-fourth

Language Arts Grade 1 Answers

Lesson 1.1 Common and Proper Nouns

A **common noun** names a person, place, or thing.
   girl (person)   school (place)   pen (thing)

A **proper noun** names a special person, place, or thing. A proper noun starts with a capital letter.

(D)ego goes to (D)avis (E)lementary.
(A)bby has a dog named (M)ilo.
When will you move to (T)exas?

Complete It
Finish each sentence below. Use a common noun from the box.

| buddy | park | ball | bench |

1. Today, Leo and I went to the __park__.
2. He is my __buddy__.
3. We played catch with my __ball__.
4. We sat on a __bench__ to drink our juice.

| Tip | The words **a**, **an** and **the** can help you find nouns.
   a swing   **an** orange   **the** moon |

82

Lesson 1.1 Common and Proper Nouns

Identify It
Look at each word in the box. If it is a proper noun, write it under **Proper Nouns**. If it is a common noun, write it under **Common Nouns**.

| man | teacher | book | Long's Toy Store |
| Ben | New York | Anna | farm |

Proper Nouns / Common Nouns

Ben / man
New York / book
Anna / teacher
Long's Toy Store / farm

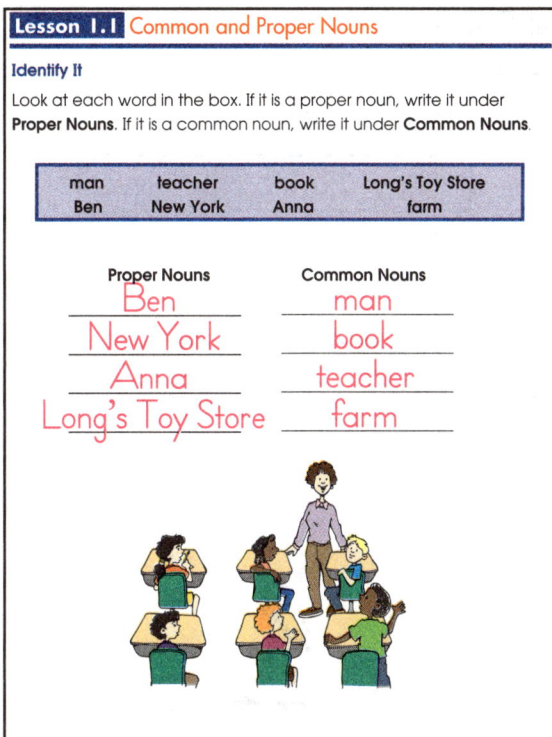

83

Lesson 1.1 Common and Proper Nouns

Sam   Miles   Amina

Rewrite It
Rewrite each sentence. Use a capital letter for each proper noun.

1. jess will go to dalton library today.
   __Jess will go to Dalton Library today.__
2. mrs. ling works at green valley hospital.
   __Mrs. Ling works at Green Valley Hospital.__
3. ted made a left turn on main street.
   __Ted made a left turn on Main Street.__

Try It
Make a list of three proper nouns from your life. You can use names of people you know. You can use places you visit. Make sure to start each one with a capital letter.

__Answers will vary.__

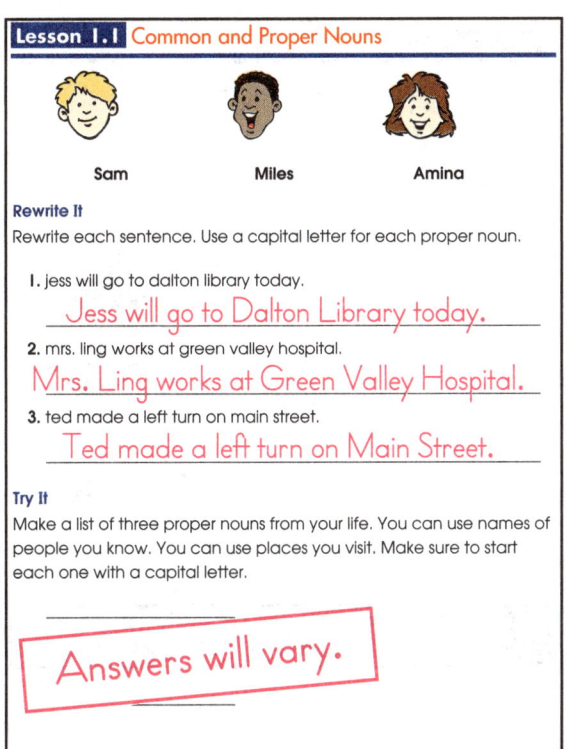

84

Lesson 1.2 Verbs

Verbs are action words. They tell what happens in a sentence.

   Jamal **drops** the ball.   Mia **laughs** at the joke.   Tim **sets** the table.

Identify It
Underline the verb in each sentence.

1. Imani and Kate <u>jump</u> rope.
2. Imani <u>counts</u>.
3. Kate <u>trips</u> on the rope.
4. Imani <u>helps</u> her friend.

Try It
Write another sentence about Imani and Kate. Underline the verb you use.

__Answers will vary.__

85

Spectrum Grade 1
287

Language Arts Grade 1 Answers

Lesson 1.2 Verbs

Rewrite It

Rewrite each sentence. Change each underlined verb to a new verb. Choose from the verbs in the box.

trims	sings	draws	bikes
walks	swims	reads	

Answers will vary. Possible answers:

1. Nico <u>skates</u> every Friday.
   Nico swims every Friday.

2. Ava <u>runs</u> home from school.
   Ava walks home from school.

3. Tess <u>dances</u> in her room.
   Tess sings in her room.

4. Jon <u>climbs</u> the trees in his yard.
   Jon trims the trees in his yard.

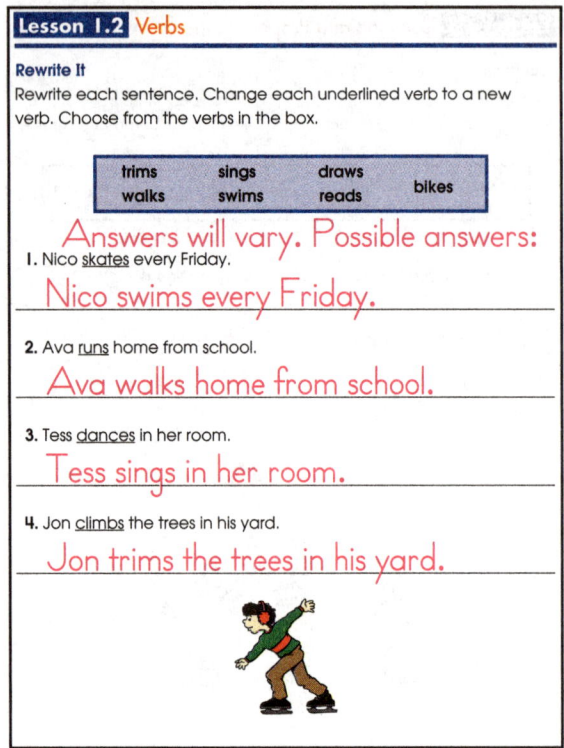

86

Lesson 1.3 Pronouns

A **pronoun** is a word that can take the place of a noun.

<u>Ella</u> paints a picture.   **She** paints a picture.
<u>Omar and I</u> like to draw.   **We** like to draw.

The words **I, me, you, he, she, him, her, it, we, us, they,** and **them** are pronouns.

Match It

Draw a line to match each word or words on the left with a pronoun on the right.

Ann — she
the crayon — it
Ben — he
Mom and Dad — they

Try It

Write one sentence using a noun. Then, rewrite it using a pronoun.

Answers will vary.

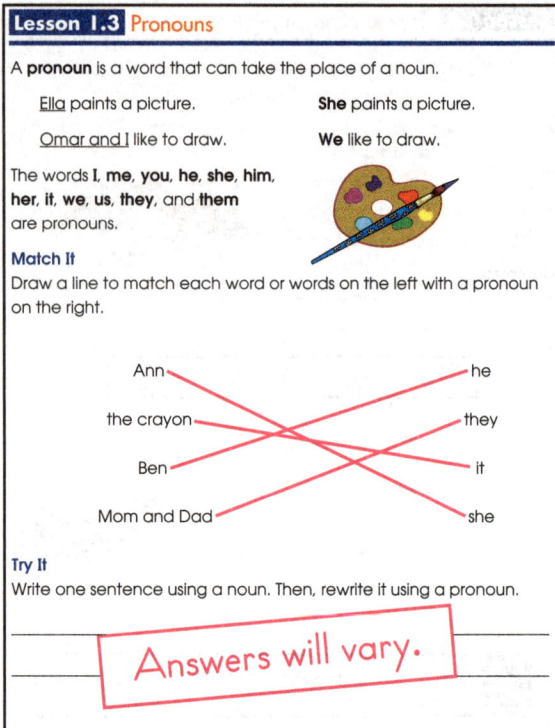

87

Lesson 1.3 Pronouns

Complete It

Read the story. Fill in each blank. Use the pronouns in the box. Make sure to start each sentence with a capital.

my	I	them	they
he	me	she	it

I love to make art. **I** hang up all my paintings in my room. Mom painted one wall with special paint. **She** said I can draw right on the wall! **My** little brothers like it, too. **They** draw while I am at school. Mom said I should let **them**. Jake drew a dinosaur for **me**. I think **it** is pretty cool. **He** wants to be an artist, too!

88

Lesson 1.4 Adjectives

An **adjective** is a word that describes a noun. It tells more about a noun. Adjectives can answer the question **What kind?**

the **yellow** duck   the **hard** rock   the **shiny** penny

Identify It

Circle the adjective in each sentence. Make a line under the noun it tells about.

Example: Samir has (brown) <u>eyes</u>.

1. Jada picked the (pink) <u>roses</u>.
2. A (tiny) <u>bee</u> buzzed around the garden.
3. Meg planted the (green) <u>sprouts</u>.
4. She wiped off her (dirty) <u>hands</u>.
5. Lex looked up at the (tall) <u>sunflower</u>.
6. What a (hot) <u>day</u>!

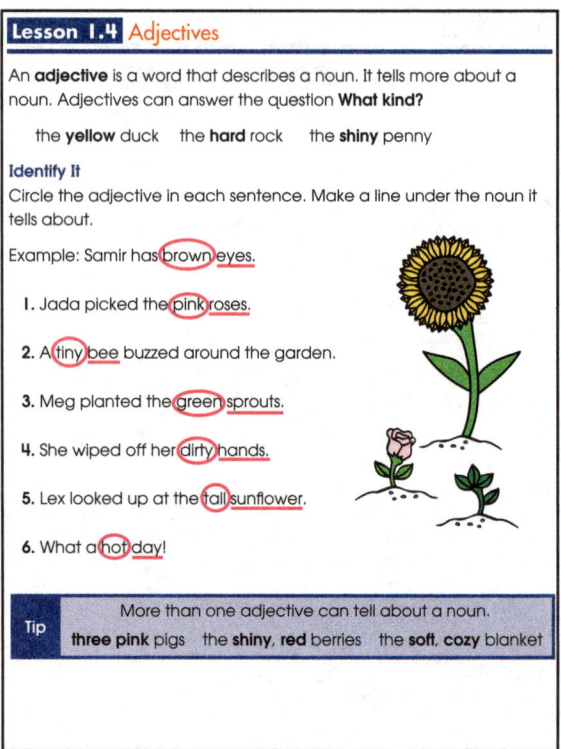

Tip	More than one adjective can tell about a noun. **three pink** pigs the **shiny, red** berries the **soft, cozy** blanket

89

Spectrum Grade 1

Language Arts Grade 1 Answers

Lesson 1.4 Adjectives

Solve It

Circle the adjectives from the box in the word search.

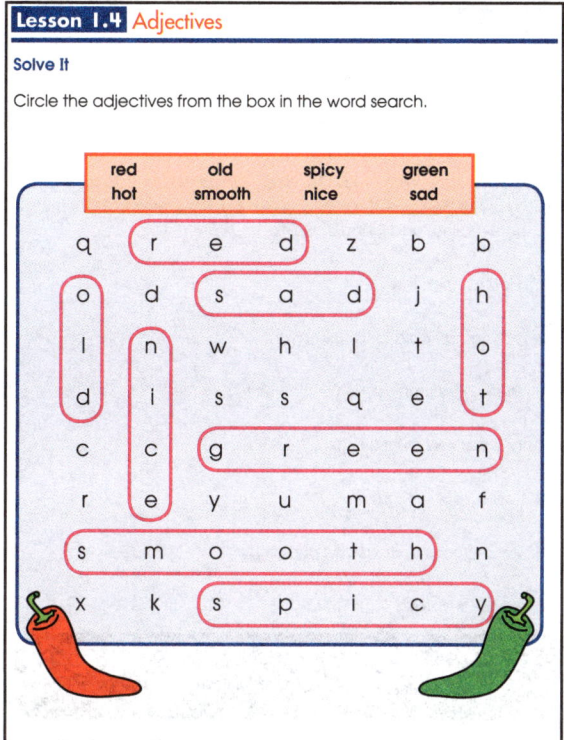

Lesson 1.5 Prepositions

A **preposition** can show location (where) or time (when). Prepositions link nouns to other words in the sentence. Some common prepositions are **to, from, in, on, behind, at, below, near, by, above, into, off,** and **with**.

Example: The book is **below** the shelf.

Identify It

Each sentence below has one preposition. Find and circle the prepositions.

1. Hal put his hat (on) his head.
2. It was cold (in) the cave!
3. Water dripped (from) the ceiling.
4. A rock fell (near) Hal's foot.
5. The cave was filled (with) bats!
6. (At) 4:00, the cave tour was done.

Lesson 1.5 Prepositions

Complete It

Use the words in the box to complete each item below.

| beside | above | in | behind | under |

1. Where is the fox? __in__ a box
2. Where is the bear? __beside__ the boy
3. Where is the girl? __under__ the covers
4. Where is the cat? __above__ the dog
5. Where is the dog house? __behind__ the dog

Try It

Write two sentences that tell where a mouse might hide. Use a preposition in each sentence.

1. Answers will vary.
2.

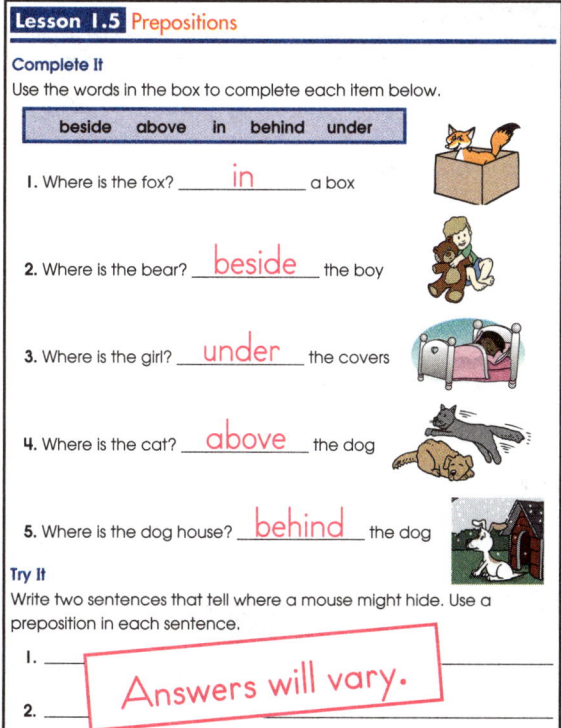

Lesson 1.6 Sentences

A **sentence** is a complete thought. It starts with a capital letter. It ends with an end mark.

(T)im plays ball(.) (T)hat book is funny(.) (L)ook at the frog(.)

Identify It

Look at each group of words. If it is a sentence, make a check mark ✓ on the line. Circle the capital letter. Circle the end mark.

1. ✓ (T)he fire truck is bright red(.)
2. ___ shiny and clean
3. ___ shows us the hoses
4. ✓ (I) can see the ladders on top(.)
5. ✓ (T)he siren is very loud(.)
6. ___ cover my ears
7. ✓ (W)e climb inside(.)

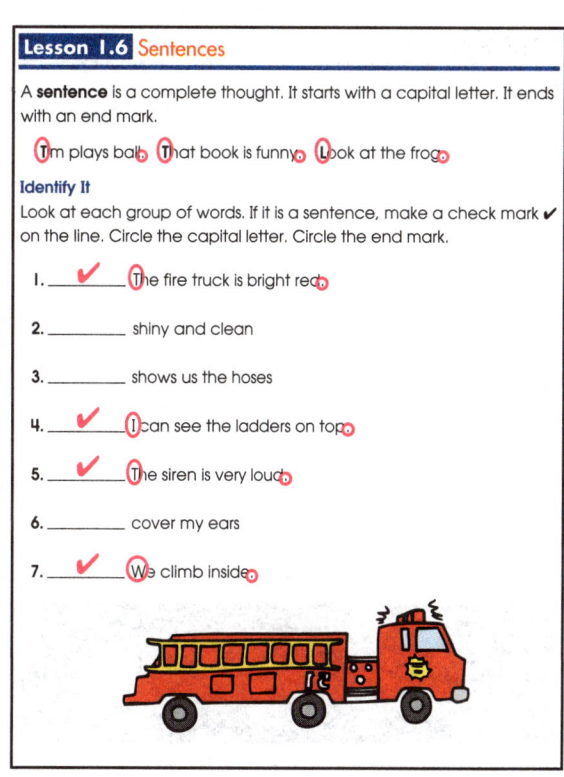

Spectrum Grade 1

Language Arts Grade 1 Answers

Lesson 1.6 Sentences

Rewrite It
Read each set of words below. Rewrite it as a sentence. Make sure to start with a capital and end with a period.

1. our fire station has a dog
   Our fire station has a dog.

2. he is white with black spots
   He is white with black spots.

3. his name is Charlie
   His name is Charlie.

4. he likes to ride in the truck
   He likes to ride in the truck.

Try It
Write two sentences about Charlie.

Answers will vary.

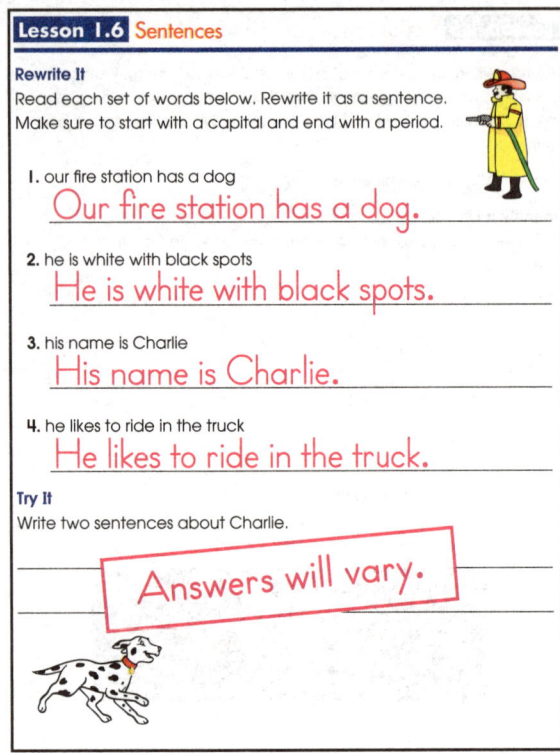

94

Lesson 1.7 Statements

A **statement** is a telling sentence. It starts with a capital letter. It ends with a period.

(A)nton is in first grade(.) (D)inner is ready(.)

Proof It
Read each statement below. If it does not start with a capital, make three lines under the letter (≡). Write the capital letter above. If the period is missing, add it and circle it.

E
ella lost her pencil(.)

L
1. look outside on a clear, dark night.

2. You will see many stars(.)

T
3. they are very far away(.)

S
4. stars do not live forever.

5. Some groups of stars have names(.)

O
6. our sun is a star(.)

95

Lesson 1.7 Statements

Rewrite It
Rewrite the sentences. Each should begin with a capital and end with a period.

1. jaya has a telescope
   Jaya has a telescope.

2. jaya likes to see the stars
   Jaya likes to see the stars.

3. she can find the Big Dipper
   She can find the Big Dipper.

4. dad showed her Venus
   Dad showed her Venus.

5. the moon is easy to spot
   The moon is easy to spot.

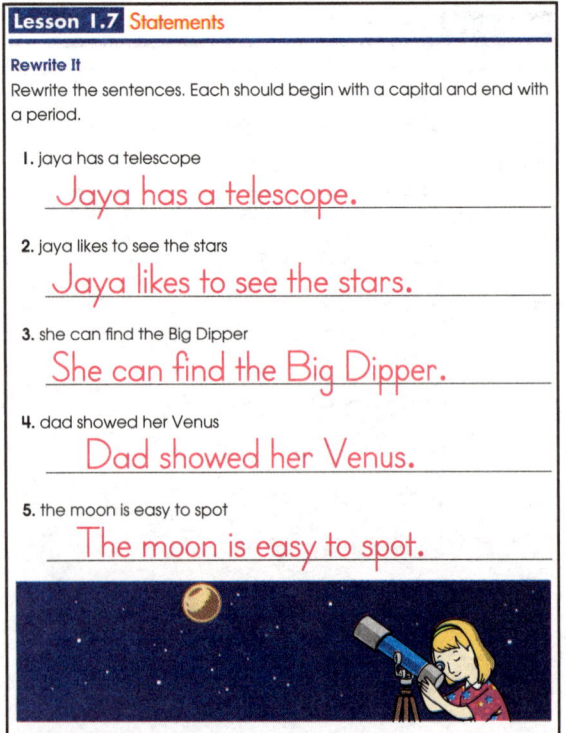

96

Lesson 1.8 Questions

A **question** is an asking sentence. A question starts with a capital letter. It ends with a question mark.

(W)here is your house(?) (W)hat time is it(?) (D)o you have a cat(?)

Complete It
Complete each question with a question mark.

1. Who was the first U.S. president ?
2. Where was George Washington born ?
3. How long was he president ?
4. Did he live in the White House ?
5. What was Washington like as a boy ?

Try It
What if you could talk to George Washington? Write two questions you would ask him.

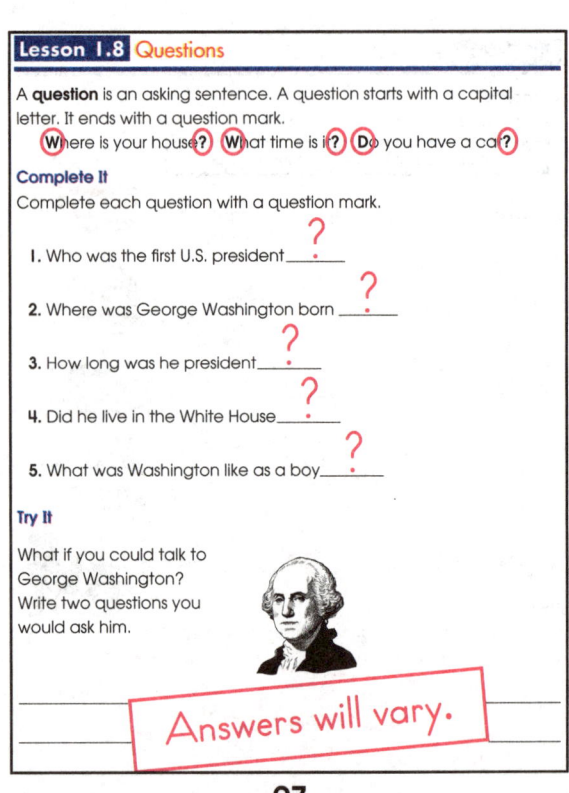

Answers will vary.

97

Spectrum Grade 1

Language Arts Grade 1 Answers

Lesson 1.8 Questions

Match It

Read each statement about the White House. Read the questions in the box. Write the letter of the question that matches each statement.

> A. How many rooms does it have?
> B. Who was first to live in it?
> C. How many chefs work there?
> D. Who named the White House?

1. __D__ Theodore Roosevelt named the White House.
2. __A__ It has 132 rooms.
3. __C__ Five chefs work at the White House.
4. __B__ John Adams was first to live in it.

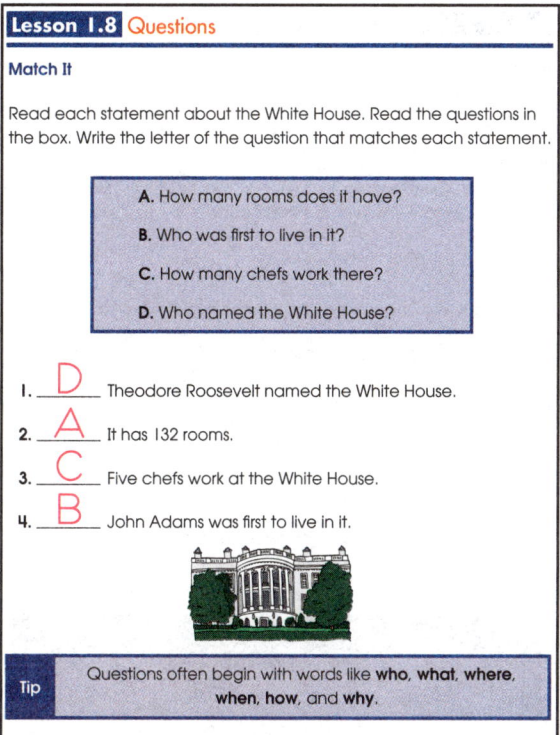

Tip Questions often begin with words like **who**, **what**, **where**, **when**, **how**, and **why**.

98

Lesson 1.9 Exclamations

An **exclamation** is a sentence that shows excitement. It can also show surprise. It starts with a capital letter. It ends with an exclamation point.

(I) need help(!) (We) won the game(!) (V)acation starts today(!)

Identify It

Read each pair of sentences. One sentence in each pair is a statement. The other sentence is an exclamation. Add the correct end marks.

1. I won the race __!__

   Today is Monday __.__

2. Finn is my best friend __.__

   Finn found ten dollars __!__

3. I have two sisters __.__

   Something is out there __!__

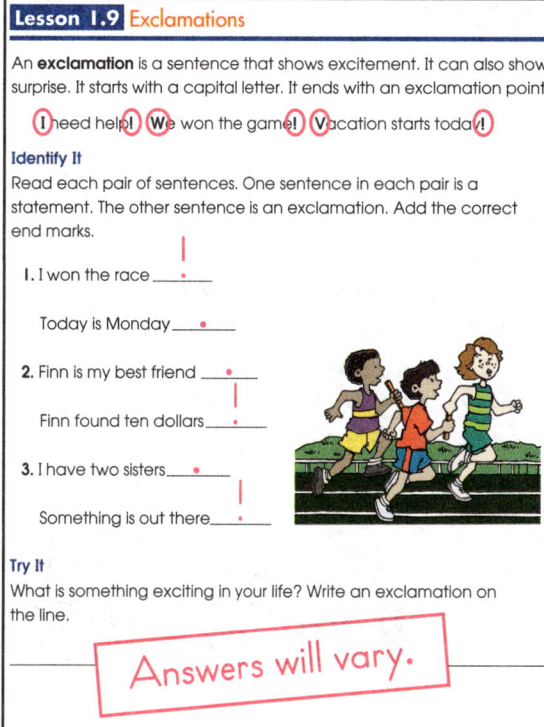

Try It

What is something exciting in your life? Write an exclamation on the line.

__Answers will vary.__

99

Lesson 1.9 Exclamations

Rewrite It

Rewrite each exclamation on the line. Remember, start with a capital. End with an exclamation point.

1. the dog got out
   __The dog got out!__

2. don't knock over your cup
   __Don't knock over your cup!__

3. lena's painting came in first place
   __Lena's painting came in first place!__

4. i lost my first tooth
   __I lost my first tooth!__

Tip Some exclamations are just one word.
Help! Wow! Great! Ouch!

100

Lesson 1.10 Combining Sentences

Sometimes, two sentences can be made into one. Both sentences must tell about the same thing.

Frogs live in the pond. Fish live in the pond.

Use the word **and** to join the parts of the sentence.

Frogs **and** fish live in the pond.

Complete It

Read the sentences.
Fill in the missing words.

1. Max went to the fair. Li went to the fair.

   Max __and__ Li went to the fair.

2. Mom rode the Ferris wheel. Dad rode the Ferris wheel.

   __Mom__ and Dad rode the Ferris wheel.

3. The juice was cold. The ice cream was cold.

   The juice and __ice cream__ were cold.

4. Li played two games. Mom played two games.

   __Li__ and Mom played two games.

101

Spectrum Grade 1

Language Arts Grade 1 Answers

Lesson 1.10 Combining Sentences

Identify It

Read the letter. Three pairs of sentences can be joined. Underline each pair.

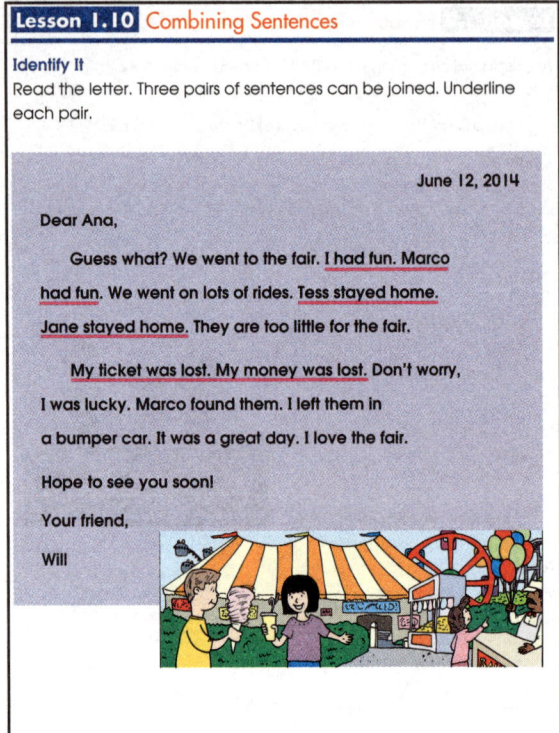

June 12, 2014

Dear Ana,

   Guess what? We went to the fair. <u>I had fun. Marco had fun.</u> We went on lots of rides. <u>Tess stayed home. Jane stayed home.</u> They are too little for the fair.

   <u>My ticket was lost. My money was lost.</u> Don't worry, I was lucky. Marco found them. I left them in a bumper car. It was a great day. I love the fair.

Hope to see you soon!

Your friend,

Will

102

Lesson 2.1 Capitalizing the First Word in a Sentence

A sentence always begins with a capital letter. This shows that a new sentence is starting.

(W)hat is your name?   (T)asha has two birds.   (I) see the train!

Proof It

Look for the words that should be capitalized. Mark the letter with three lines below it (≡). Then, write the capital above it.

Example: <u>s</u>onya will wear her red dress. [S]

   <u>B</u>ats are odd animals. They fly like birds. <u>E</u>ven so, they are not birds. Bats are mammals, like dogs and cats. <u>M</u>ost bats eat bugs. <u>S</u>ome eat fruit.

   Bats sleep during the day. <u>T</u>hey are awake at night. They do not see well. They make a very high sound. <u>T</u>he sound bounces off things. This tells bats where things are. <u>I</u>t helps them get around.

103

Lesson 2.1 Capitalizing the First Word in a Sentence

Rewrite It

Rewrite each sentence. Make sure to begin with a capital letter.

1. last week, a bat got in our house.
   Last week, a bat got in our house.

2. i didn't know what it was at first.
   I didn't know what it was at first.

3. mom caught it and let it go outside.
   Mom caught it and let it go outside.

4. that poor bat was scared!
   That poor bat was scared!

5. i don't think he'll be back.
   I don't think he'll be back.

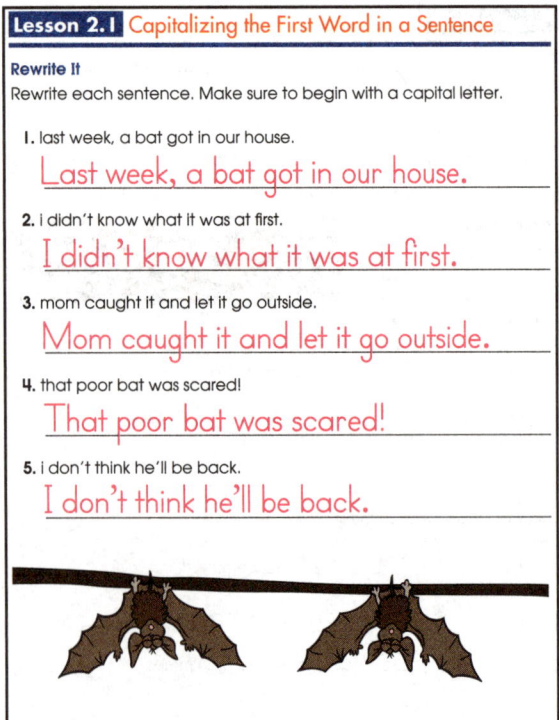

104

Lesson 2.2 Capitalizing the Pronoun I

The pronoun **I** is always capitalized. It can start a sentence. It can be in the middle of a sentence.

(I) like pears.   (I) will wear a jacket.   Min and (I) want to swing.

Proof It

Read the story. Each time you see the word **I**, make sure it is capitalized. If it is not, make three lines below it (≡). Then, write the capital above it.

Example: Lulu and <u>i</u> went on a walk. [I]

   Last week, <u>i</u> went to the dentist. I was not nervous. <u>i</u> was just getting a check-up. My sister had a tooth pulled once. Grace and <u>i</u> were playing outside. She tripped and hit her mouth. I knew she needed help, so <u>i</u> called for Mom. Mom and <u>i</u> took Grace right to Dr. Cruz. <u>i</u> told him what happened. Then, Mom and I sat with Grace. She was so brave! Her lip was puffy, but she was okay. Grace and <u>i</u> will be more careful from now on!

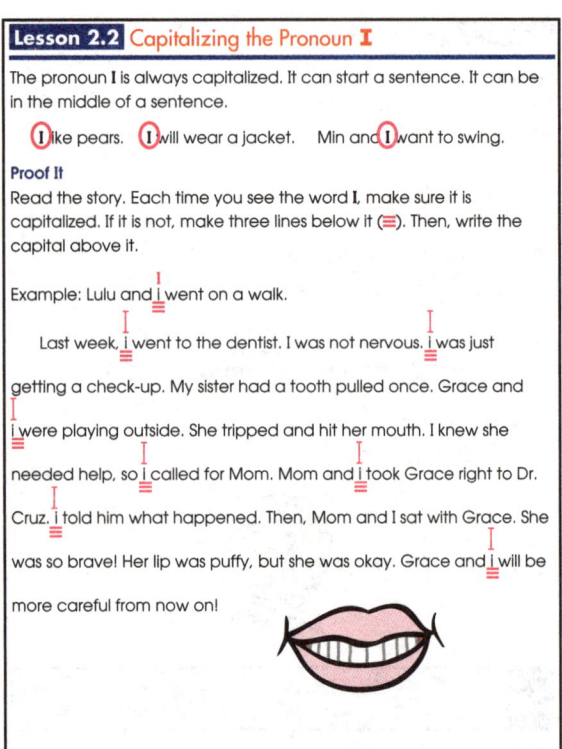

105

Spectrum Grade 1

Language Arts Grade 1 Answers

Lesson 2.2 Capitalizing the Pronoun **I**

Try It
Read each sentence below. Write the word **I** in the box. Fill in the other blank with a word that finishes the sentence.

1. [I] like to eat _Answers will vary_.
2. _Answers will vary_ and [I] play catch.
3. [I] like the color _Answers will vary_.
4. Each weekend, [I] go _Answers will vary_.
5. My _Answers will vary_ and [I] like to read books together.
6. [I] have a cool _Answers will vary_.

106

Lesson 2.3 Capitalizing Names

Names begin with a capital letter. A person's name starts with a capital letter. A pet's name starts with a capital letter, too.

My sister's name is (E)mma.   I have a cat named (S)ocks.

Match It
The child and pet in each picture need a name. Choose a set of names from the box. Write them next to the picture. Make sure you start each name with a capital letter.

| lily and lucky | carlos and coco | |
| ben and bubbles | greg and gus | stella and star |

Order of answers will vary.

107

Lesson 2.3 Capitalizing Names

Proof It
The names below do not start with a capital letter. Find each letter that should be a capital letter. Make three lines below it (≡). Then, write the capital letter above it.

1. L̲ J̲ S̲ — l̲uke, j̲ay, and Leo are all s̲am's brothers.
2. B̲ S̲ — Lu named the kittens b̲ella and s̲assy.
3. A̲ — Jack saw his friend a̲va at the park.
4. J̲ M̲ — j̲ess got to milk m̲illie and Bonnie at the farm.

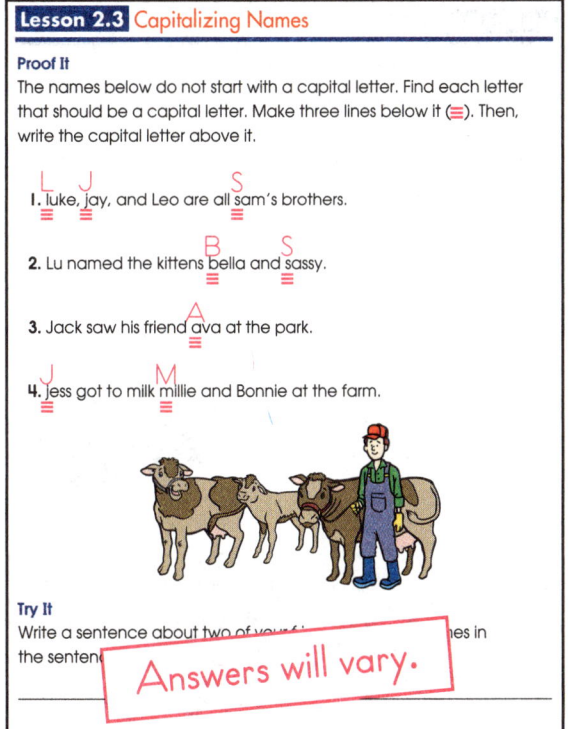

Try It
Write a sentence about two of your friends. Use their names in the sentence.

Answers will vary.

108

Lesson 2.4 Capitalizing Place Names

Place names begin with a capital letter.

(D)anville, (K)entucky   (C)love (L)ibrary
(M)aple (S)treet   (J)ackson (S)chool
(V)enus   (J)apan

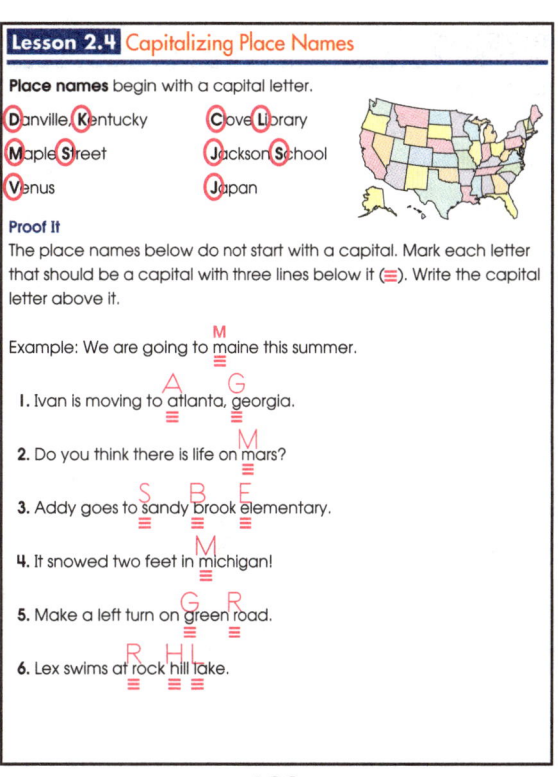

Proof It
The place names below do not start with a capital. Mark each letter that should be a capital with three lines below it (≡). Write the capital letter above it.

Example: We are going to m̲aine this summer.

1. Ivan is moving to a̲tlanta, g̲eorgia.
2. Do you think there is life on m̲ars?
3. Addy goes to s̲andy b̲rook e̲lementary.
4. It snowed two feet in m̲ichigan!
5. Make a left turn on g̲reen r̲oad.
6. Lex swims at r̲ock h̲ill l̲ake.

109

Spectrum Grade 1
293

Language Arts Grade 1 Answers

Lesson 2.4 Capitalizing Place Names

Try It
Answer each question. Make sure to start each place name with a capital letter.

1. What is the name of your street?
2. What city were you born in?
3. What is a state you would like to visit?
4. What country do you live in?
5. What is the name of a place you go a lot? It could be a school. Maybe it is a store or a library.

Answers will vary.

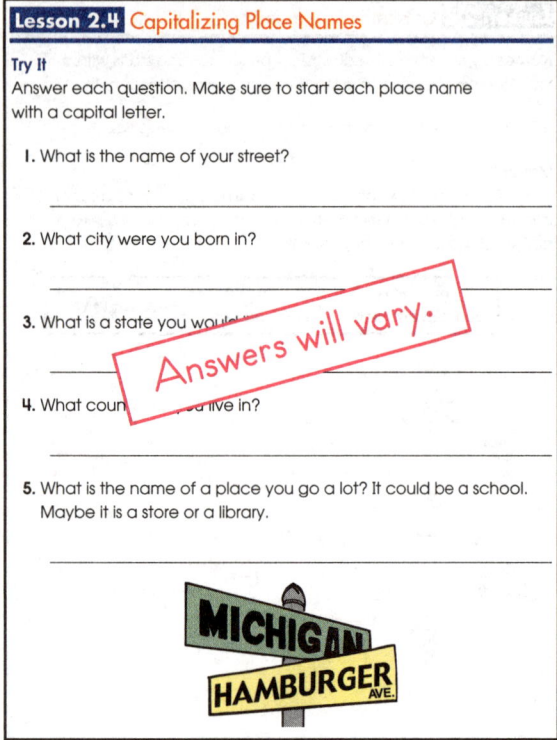

110

Lesson 2.5 Capitalizing Days and Months

The **days of the week** start with a capital letter.
(M)onday, (T)uesday, (W)ednesday, (Th)ursday, (F)riday, (S)aturday, Sunday

The **months of the year** start with a capital letter, too.
(J)anuary, February, (M)arch, (A)pril, (M)ay, (J)une, July, (A)ugust, (S)eptember, (O)ctober, (N)ovember, (D)ecember

Solve It
Read each clue. Write the day of the week that matches it. Use the list above.

1. People like me a lot. I am the first day of the weekend. **Saturday**
2. I am the first weekday. My name starts with **m**. **Monday**
3. You can find the word **sun** hiding in my name. **Sunday**
4. I am the last weekday. Here comes the weekend! **Friday**
5. I come in the middle of the week. My name starts with **w**. **Wednesday**
6. My name starts with **t**. I come near the end of the week. **Thursday**
7. My name starts with **t**, too. I come near the start of the week. **Tuesday**

111

Lesson 2.5 Capitalizing Days and Months

Complete It
Fill in the month in each sentence. Make sure to use a capital letter.

1. (june) Julia's birthday is in **June**.
2. (april) Andy ate apples in **April**.
3. (july) Jake plays jacks in **July**.
4. (may) Mira met Matt in **May**.
5. (october) Olly saw an owl in **October**.
6. (september) Sam swam in **September**.

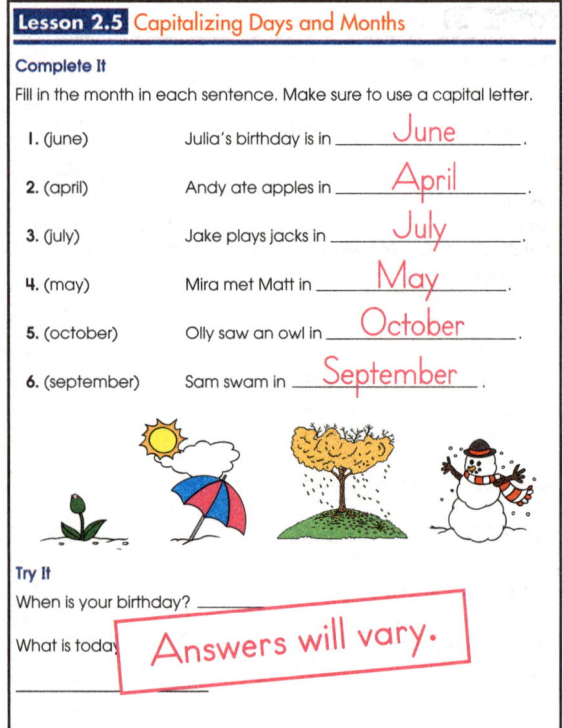

Try It
When is your birthday?
What is today's date?

Answers will vary.

112

Lesson 2.6 Periods

A **period** is an end mark. It comes at the end of a sentence.
I have a hole in my pants(.) Luis has a loose tooth(.)

Complete It
Each sentence below is missing a period. Add it and circle it.

Example: Turn on the lights(.)

1. Giant pandas are found in China(.)
2. They live in the mountains(.)
3. There are not many pandas left in the wild(.)
4. Pandas have black rings around their eyes(.)
5. They can weigh 250 pounds(.)
6. Pandas eat bamboo(.)
7. They get most of their water from bamboo(.)

Try It
Look at the picture of the panda above. Write a sentence about it. Make sure it ends with a period.

Answers will vary.

113

Spectrum Grade 1

Language Arts Grade 1 Answers

Lesson 2.6 Periods

Tip: A capital letter can show you where a new sentence starts.

Proof It
The periods are missing in the paragraph. Add them and circle them.

Baby pandas are called cubs. A new baby is very small. It is about the size of a stick of butter. The cubs are not black and white. They are pink. A new cub looks more like a mouse than a bear. It has almost no hair.

A baby panda can not do much at first. The baby's eyes stay shut for 6 to 8 weeks. It takes a few months for a cub to learn to walk. Baby pandas need their moms, just like baby humans.

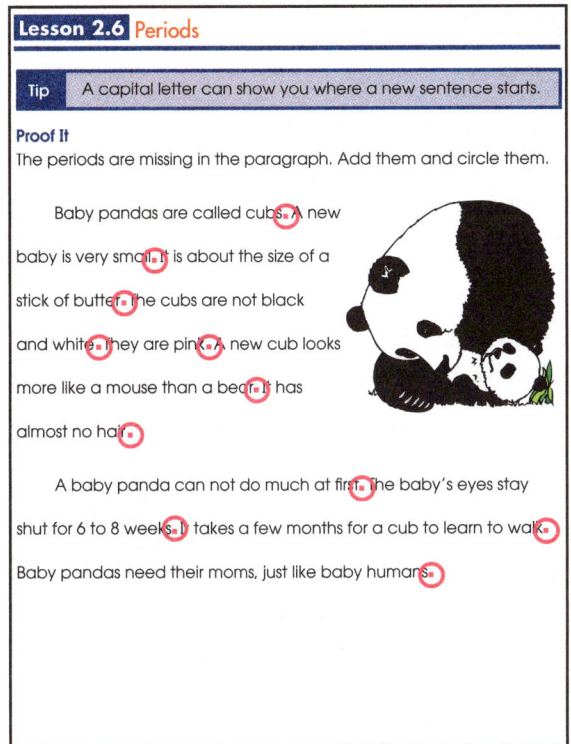

114

Lesson 2.7 Question Marks

A **question mark** comes at the end of a question. It shows where the question ends.

Can you play checkers? Where is my red bow? Have you seen Erin?

Rewrite It
Rewrite each question. Make sure it starts with a capital letter and ends with a question mark.

1. where are you moving
   Where are you moving?

2. have you packed yet
   Have you packed yet?

3. who will drive the moving van
   Who will drive the moving van?

4. what color is your new house
   What color is your new house?

5. how far away is it
   How far away is it?

115

Lesson 2.7 Question Marks

Identify It
Read each pair of sentences. Add a period after each statement. Add a question mark after each question. Underline the word that tells you the sentence is a question.

1. <u>What</u> is your new address?
   It is 811 Elm Street.

2. I can't find my roller skates.
   <u>Have</u> you seen them?

3. <u>What</u> school do you go to?
   I go to Shady Lane School.

4. Nick and Izzy live next door.
   <u>Who</u> lives in the blue house?

5. <u>Why</u> are you moving?
   My mom got a new job.

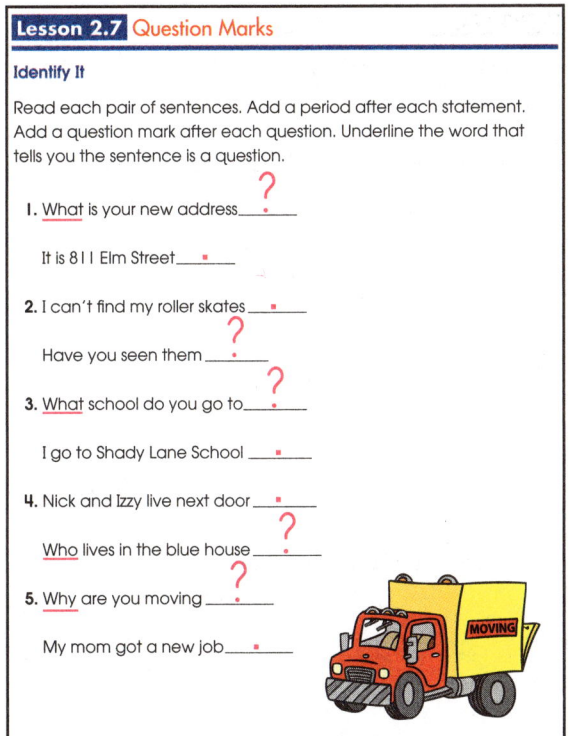

116

Lesson 2.8 Exclamation Points

An **exclamation point** comes at the end of an exclamation. An exclamation is a sentence that shows excitement. It can also show surprise.

That's great news! Look at the snake! We won!

Identify It
Read each pair of sentences. Add a period after each statement. Add an exclamation point after each exclamation.

1. Today is Saturday.
   It rained four inches today!

2. Don't forget your umbrella!
   Jon has a green umbrella.

3. Watch out for that branch!
   Dad will pick up the branches.

4. Jaya did not step in the puddle.
   My book fell in the puddle!

117

Spectrum Grade 1

Language Arts Grade 1 Answers

Lesson 2.8 Exclamation Points

Try It

Look at each picture. Write an exclamation to go with it. Begin with a capital letter. End with an exclamation point.

Answers will vary.

118

Lesson 2.9 Commas with Dates

A **comma** is a punctuation mark. In a date, it goes between the day and the year.

June 20, 1973   October 1, 2006   April 4, 1866

If a comma is missing, use this mark (∧) to add it.

March 17∧2014

Proof It

Commas are missing from the dates below. Use this mark (∧) to add them.

1. John moved to New York on December 23∧1982.
2. Aunt Keiko was born on February 19∧1979.
3. Grandma and Grandpa got married on May 6∧1960.
4. I met Jada on July 11∧2008.
5. Riley's birthday is August 14∧2004.

Try It

When were you born? Write the date on the line. _____

Ask a friend when he or she was born. Write the date on the line.
_____

119

Lesson 2.9 Commas with Dates

Rewrite It

Rewrite each date. Use commas where they are needed.

1. January 5 1984 — January 5, 1984
2. November 18 2002 — November 18, 2002
3. May 23 1999 — May 23, 1999
4. February 9 2015 — February 9, 2015
5. July 31 1944 — July 31, 1944
6. September 12 1965 — September 12, 1965
7. April 29 1814 — April 29, 1814

120

Lesson 2.10 Commas with Cities and States

A **comma** is used between the name of a city and state.

Detroit, Michigan   Wilmington, Delaware   Portland, Oregon

Proof It

Add a comma between each city and state. Use this mark (∧) to add each comma.

1. You may have heard of Chicago∧Illinois.
2. You might know Dallas∧Texas.
3. Have you heard of Chicken∧Alaska?
4. Would you like to go to Bumble Bee∧Arizona?
5. How about Two Egg∧Florida?
6. Is it boring to live in Boring∧Maryland?
7. What is it like in Moon∧Virginia?

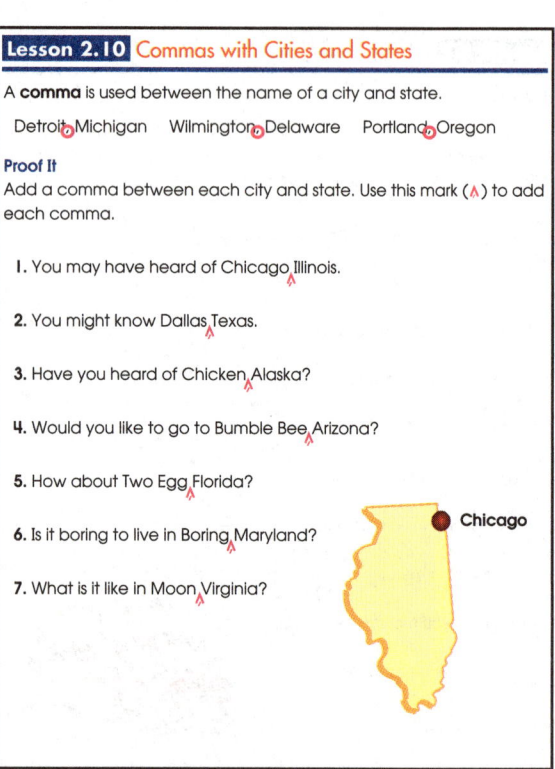

121

Spectrum Grade 1

Language Arts Grade 1 Answers

Lesson 2.10 Commas with Cities and States

Complete It
Finish each sentence with a city and state from the box. Use commas where they are needed.

Order of answers will vary.

1. Anton is moving to **Lima, Ohio**.
2. In May, Izzy will go to **Macon, Georgia**.
3. Lee's aunt lives in **Reno, Nevada**.
4. It will take Cam two days to drive to **Portland, Maine**.
5. Dan found **Austin, Texas** on the map.
6. Jane has lived in **Miami, Florida** for 11 years.

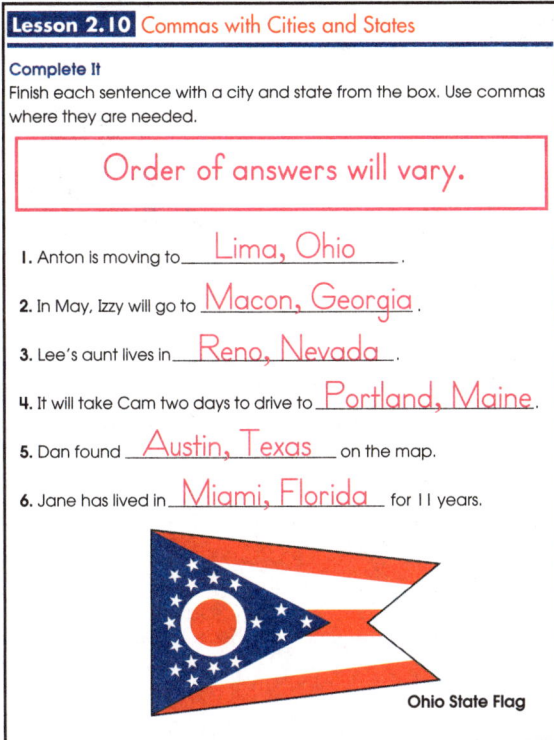

Ohio State Flag

122

Lesson 2.11 Apostrophes with Possessives

An **apostrophe** plus **s** (**'s**) shows that someone owns something.

Keisha**'s** book   Meg**'s** brush   Cody**'s** train

Complete It
Add **'s** to each blank below. Make a line under the item each person owns.

1. Emma **'s** drawing
2. Diego **'s** pen
3. Mr. Stein **'s** truck
4. Dante **'s** leaf
5. Kat **'s** frog
6. Jen **'s** apple

Try It
Write a sentence about something a friend owns. Use **'s** to show what he or she owns.

Answers will vary.

123

Lesson 2.11 Apostrophes with Possessives

Identify It
Read each pair of sentences. Make a check mark ✔ next to the one that is correct.

1. ✔ Mia's hat
   ___ Mias hat
2. ___ Blakes bird'
   ✔ Blake's bird
3. ✔ Amad's boots
   ___ Amads boots
4. ___ Rosas muffin
   ✔ Rosa's muffin
5. ___ Nicks snake'
   ✔ Nick's snake

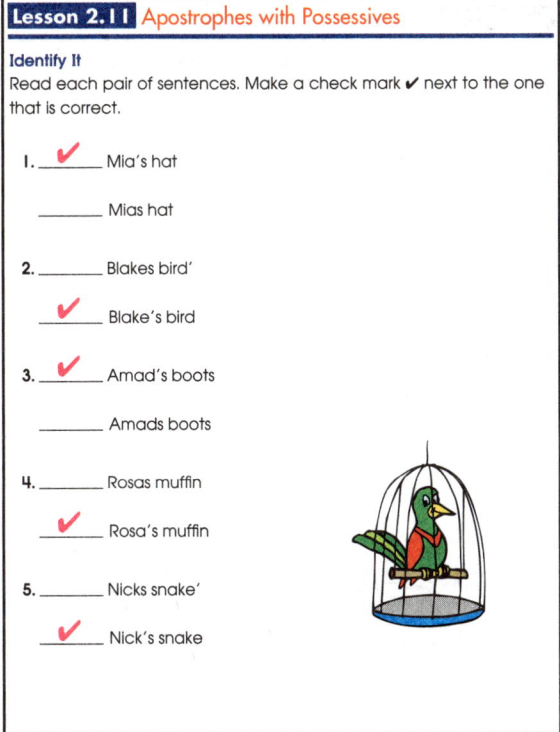

124

Lesson 3.1 Subject-Verb Agreement

When a sentence is about one person or thing, add **s** to the verb.

Jim drop**s** the ball.   The leaf blow**s** away.

When a sentence is about more than one person or thing, do not add **s**.

The cats look for mice.   Jeff and Yoko play the piano.

Match It
Draw a line to match each sentence to the correct ending.

1. Ms. Ito — grades the tests.
   grade the tests.
2. The pencils — fall on the floor.
   falls on the floor.
3. The bell — ring at 3:00.
   rings at 3:00.
4. The girls — paints in the art room.
   paint in the art room.
5. Caleb — sings after school.
   sing after school.

125

Spectrum Grade 1
297

Language Arts Grade 1 Answers

Lesson 3.1 Subject-Verb Agreement

Complete It
Circle the word that completes each sentence.

1. Max (**puts**, put) on his space suit.
2. He (slip, **slips**) on the boots.
3. The helmet (roll, **rolls**) across the floor.
4. Max and his dog (**travel**, travels) to outer space.
5. They (sees, **see**) Earth from far above.
6. Max's mom (**calls**, call) him home for dinner.

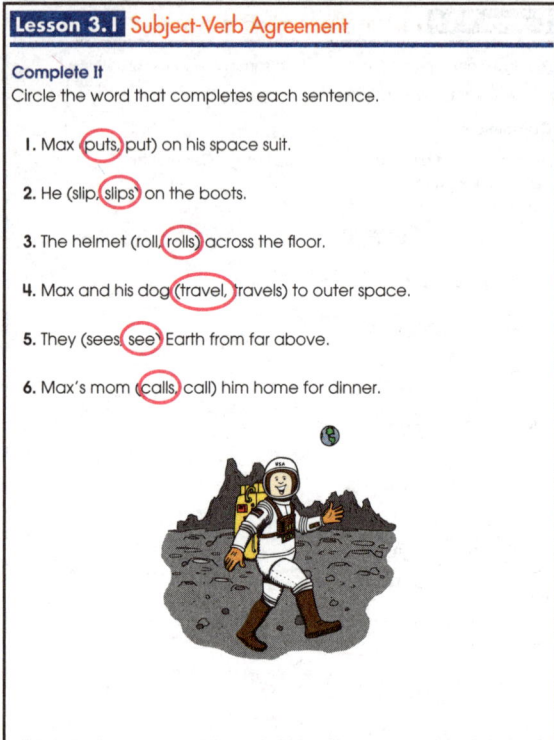

126

Lesson 3.2 Irregular Verbs: Am, Is, Are

The words **am**, **is**, and **are** are all verbs.
Use **am** with the word **I**.

  I **am** happy.   I **am** cold.

Use **is** with one person or thing.

  The balloon **is** red.   Seth **is** at the park.

Use **are** with more than one person or thing.

  The pens **are** in my desk.   The boys **are** inside.

Rewrite It
Each sentence below has the wrong verb. Rewrite it with the correct verb. Choose from **is**, **am**, or **are**.

1. The farmer am ready to milk the cows.
   The farmer is ready to milk the cows.
2. I is glad to help Bill.
   I am glad to help Bill.
3. The horse are brown and white.
   The horse is brown and white.
4. The kids is by the pond.
   The kids are by the pond.

127

Lesson 3.2 Irregular Verbs: Am, Is, Are

Complete It
Complete each sentence with the correct word from the box. Write it on the line.

1. [is are] The pig ___is___ in the mud.
2. [am are] I ___am___ sure I let the dog out.
3. [is are] The ducks ___are___ with their babies.
4. [am is] The cow ___is___ next to the fence.
5. [are is] Farmer Bill and Henry ___are___ in the kitchen.
6. [is are] The pony ___is___ six months old.

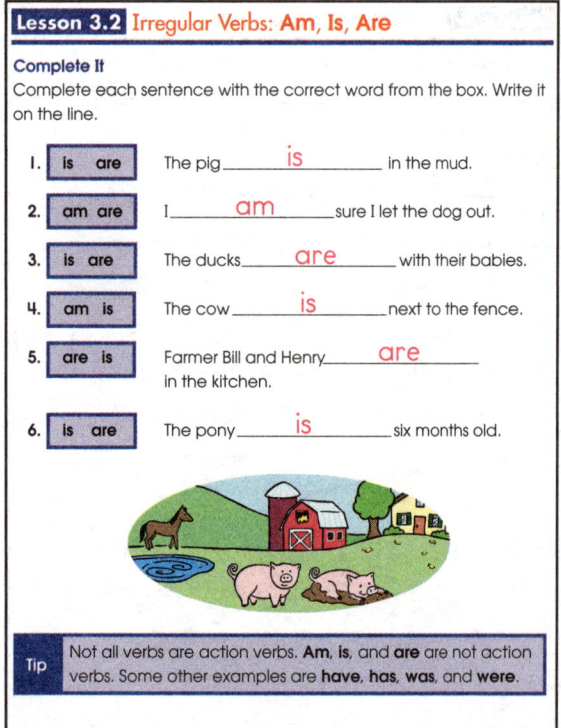

Tip: Not all verbs are action verbs. **Am**, **is**, and **are** are not action verbs. Some other examples are **have**, **has**, **was**, and **were**.

128

Lesson 3.3 Past-Tense Verbs: Was, Were

The words **was** and **were** tell about something that happened in the past.

Use **was** with one person or thing.

  The bike **was** broken.   I **was** ready for dinner.

Use **were** with more than one person or thing.

  Amit and Liza **were** at the movies.   The books **were** in the car.

Proof It
Read each sentence. Check to see if the verbs **was** and **were** are correct. If you find a mistake, cross it out. Write the correct word above it.

Example: The worm ~~were~~ **was** under the leaf.

1. The parade ~~were~~ **was** at 1:00.
2. The kids ~~was~~ **were** excited to see it.
3. The balloons were red, yellow, and green.
4. The band ~~were~~ **was** very loud.
5. Drew and Maggy ~~was~~ **were** in the first float.

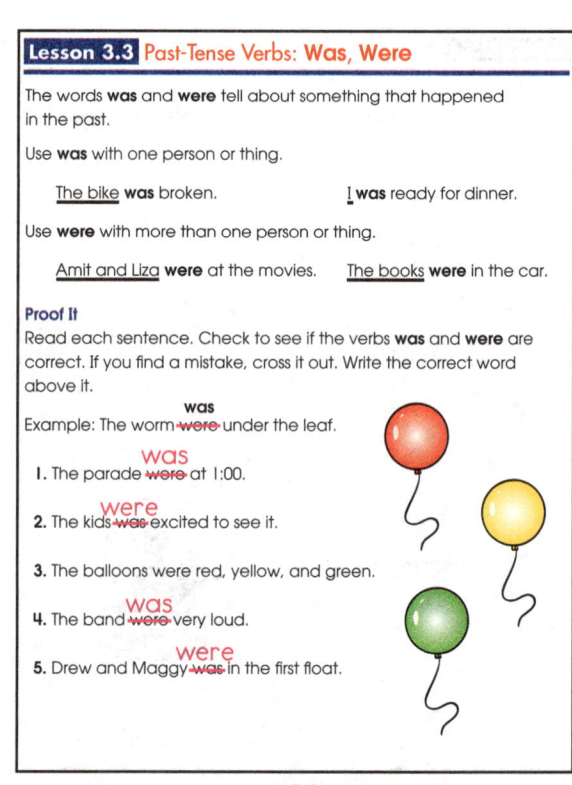

129

Spectrum Grade 1

Language Arts Grade 1 Answers

Lesson 3.3 Past-Tense Verbs: **Was, Were**

Complete It
Fill in each blank with **was** or **were**.

1. The drums **were** in the middle of the parade.
2. It **was** a sunny day.
3. We **were** lucky it didn't rain.
4. Mom and Dad **were** on the sidewalk.
5. Nico **was** the leader.
6. At the end of the parade, we **were** tired!

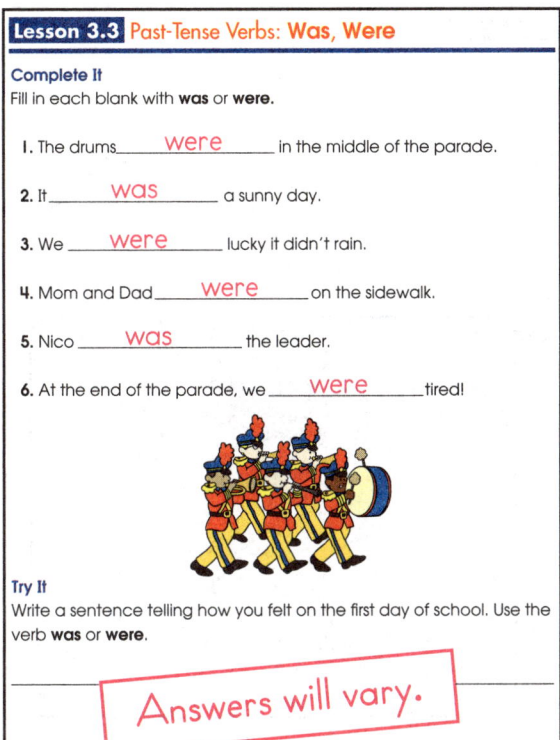

Try It
Write a sentence telling how you felt on the first day of school. Use the verb **was** or **were**.

Answers will vary.

130

Lesson 3.4 Past Tense: Add **ed**

Verbs in the **past tense** tell about things that already happened. Add **ed** to most verbs to tell about the past.

It start**ed** to rain. Henry knock**ed** on the door.

If a verb ends in **e**, just add **d**.

live → lived race → raced

Identify It
Circle the past-tense verb in each sentence.

1. The game (started) at 3:00.
2. A ball (landed) right next to me!
3. I (picked) it up.
4. The crowd (cheered).
5. The game (ended) with a score of 4 to 3.

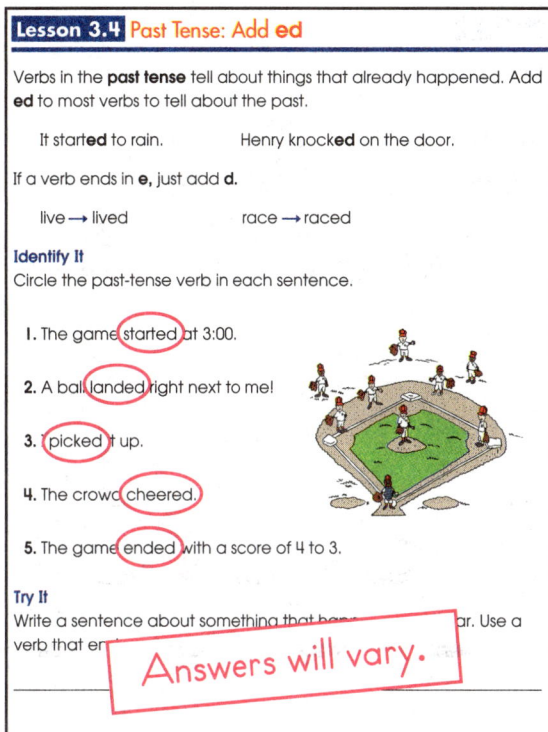

Try It
Write a sentence about something that happened. Use a verb that ends in ed.

Answers will vary.

131

Lesson 3.4 Past Tense: Add **ed**

Complete It
Complete each sentence with the verb in the box. Add **d** or **ed** to put it in the past tense.

1. look — The pitcher **looked** at the batter.
2. wait — We **waited** to see the hit.
3. race — The player **raced** to first base.
4. jump — Number 3 **jumped** up to catch the ball.
5. sail — The ball **sailed** over the fence.
6. smile — I **smiled** at my brother.
7. want — We **wanted** to see a great game, and we did!

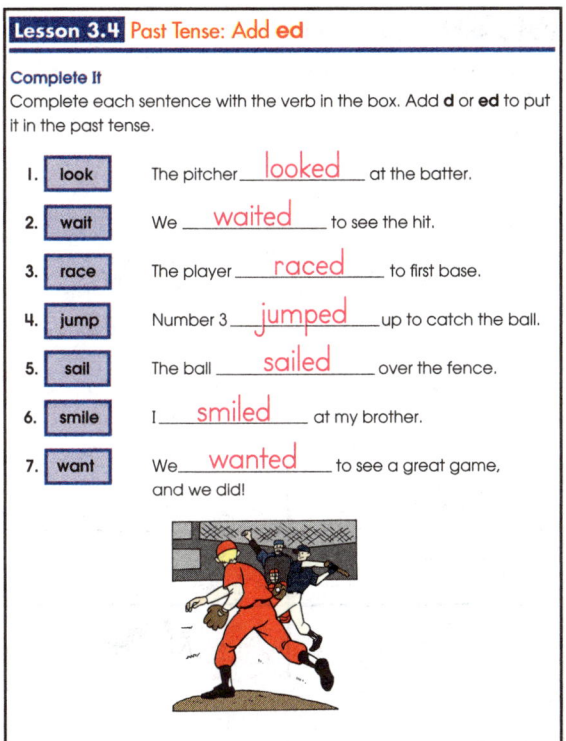

132

Lesson 3.5 Contractions with **Not**

A **contraction** is a way to join two words together. It is a shorter way to say something. An apostrophe (') takes the place of the missing letters.

Here are some contractions with **not**.

is not = isn't are not = aren't
was not = wasn't were not = weren't
does not = doesn't did not = didn't
have not = haven't can not = can't

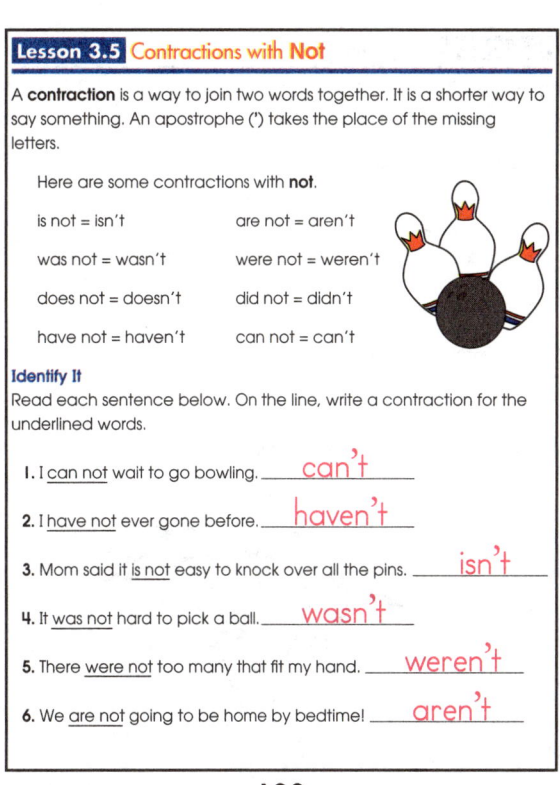

Identify It
Read each sentence below. On the line, write a contraction for the underlined words.

1. I <u>can not</u> wait to go bowling. **can't**
2. I <u>have not</u> ever gone before. **haven't**
3. Mom said it <u>is not</u> easy to knock over all the pins. **isn't**
4. It <u>was not</u> hard to pick a ball. **wasn't**
5. There <u>were not</u> too many that fit my hand. **weren't**
6. We <u>are not</u> going to be home by bedtime! **aren't**

133

Spectrum Grade 1
299

Language Arts Grade 1 Answers

Lesson 3.5 Contractions with Not

Match it
Draw a line to match each pair of words to its contraction.

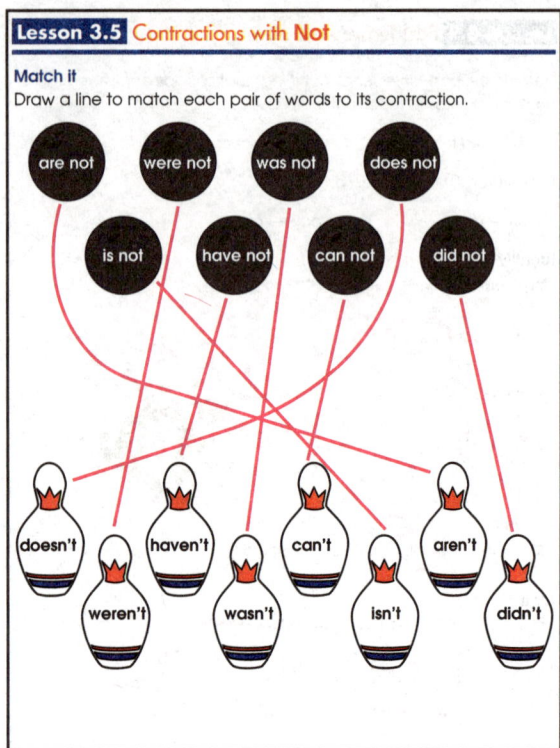

134

Lesson 3.6 Plurals with s

Plural means **more than one**. To make most nouns plural, just add **s**.
- one hand → two hands
- one plane → four planes
- one tent → six tents
- one hen → twelve hens

Solve It
Write the plural of each word on the line. Then, circle the plurals in the puzzle.

bug — bugs spider — spiders
beetle — beetles cricket — crickets
wasp — wasps ant — ants

135

Lesson 3.6 Plurals with s

Complete It
Add an **s** to each noun to make it plural.

1. Sanj found three ladybug**s**.
2. Draw that moth with your marker**s**.
3. Did you see the bee**s** fly back to their hive?
4. Jose saw four slug**s** in the garden.
5. Our dog**s** get fleas every summer.
6. Watch out for tick**s** in the woods!
7. Five inchworm**s** crawled up the leaf.

136

Lesson 3.7 Irregular Plural Nouns

For some words, do not add **s** to make the plural. Instead, the whole word changes.

One	More Than One
goose	geese
man	men
woman	women
tooth	teeth
child	children
mouse	mice
foot	feet

Other words do not change at all. Use the same word for one and more than one.

- one deer → five deer
- one fish → ten fish
- one sheep → three sheep
- one moose → eight moose

Look at each picture. Circle the word that names the picture.

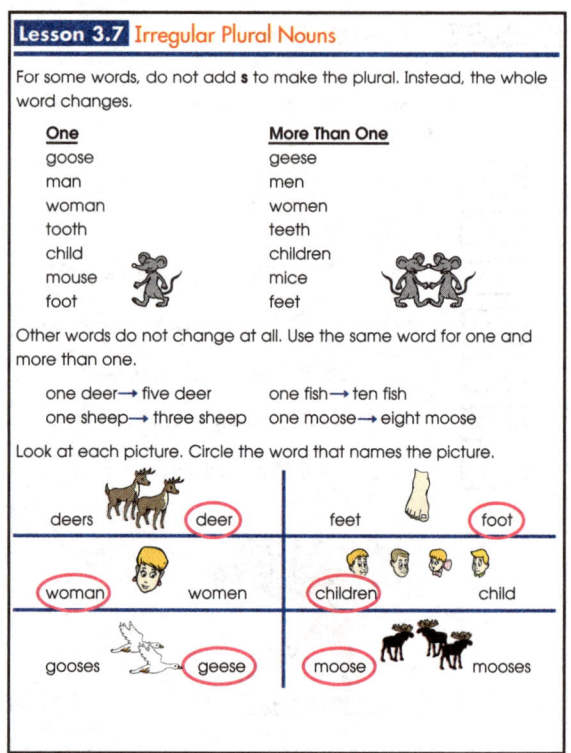

137

Spectrum Grade 1

Language Arts Grade 1 Answers

Lesson 3.7 Irregular Plural Nouns

Solve It
Look at each number and picture below. Fill in the missing word on the line. Choose from the words in the box.

mouse	men	fish
sheep	mice	teeth

4 — men
6 — teeth
1 — mouse
50 — sheep
17 — fish
22 — mice

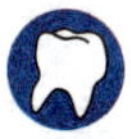

138

Lesson 3.8 Prefixes and Suffixes

A **prefix** is added to the beginning of a root word. It changes the word's meaning.

The prefix **un** means **not** or **opposite of**.
Example: **un**healthy = **not** healthy

The prefix **re** means **again**.
Example: **re**wash = wash **again**

A **suffix** is added to the end of a root word. It changes the word's meaning.

The suffix **er** means **one who**.
Example: bak**er** = one who bakes

The suffix **ed** means that something happened **in the past**. (Remember, if a word ends in **e**, just add **d**).
Example: Yesterday, Luis wash**ed** the dog.

Match It
On the line, write a word with a prefix to match each meaning.

1. read again= reread
2. opposite of dress= undress
3. not sure= unsure
4. copy again= recopy
5. told again= retell
6. not able= unable
7. fill again= refill

139

Lesson 3.8 Prefixes and Suffixes

Complete It
Each **bold** word is missing a suffix. Add the suffix **er** or **ed**. Use the meaning of the sentence to decide which one to add.

1. Riley wants to be a **paint**_er_ one day.
2. Kris **smile**_d_ at the baby.
3. Lena **tuck**_ed_ her doll into bed.
4. The **catch**_er_ stands behind home plate.
5. Mom handed a check to the **bank**_er_.

Sort the words in the box. Write them under the correct headings.

reuse	liked	unhurt	farmer
singer	resell	fixed	unfair

Words with Prefixes: reuse, unhurt, resell, unfair
Words with Suffixes: liked, farmer, singer, fixed

140

Lesson 3.9 Pronouns **I** and **Me**

You use the words **I** and **me** to talk about yourself.

   I like bananas.   Amit gave me a new book.

When you talk about yourself and another person, put them first.

   Devon and I ride the bus.   Eli made dinner for **Dad and me**.

Identify It
Circle **I** or **me** for each sentence.

1. (I, me) take piano lessons on Tuesdays.
2. Ms. Hawk gave (I, me) a gold star today.
3. (I, me) like to sing and play.
4. Mom asked (I, me) to play for Aunt Clare.
5. Aunt Clare told (I, me) that I play very well.
6. (I, me) want to play in a recital this spring.

141

Spectrum Grade 1
301

Language Arts Grade 1 Answers

Lesson 3.9 Pronouns I and Me

Complete It
Read the story. Write **I** or **me** in each blank to complete the sentences.

__I__ play the violin. My grandma gave __me__ one. It was hers. __I__ have a picture of her playing it. She told __me__ to practice every day.

My friend Avi and __I__ take lessons. I started when __I__ was three. He and __I__ like to play together. He told __me__ he wants to play the piano, too. My grandma says she can teach Avi and __me__.

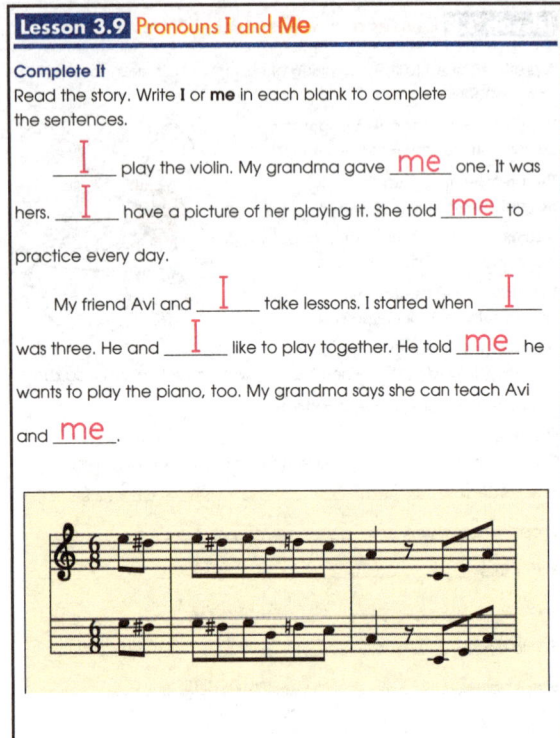

142

Lesson 3.10 Comparative Adjectives

Some adjectives are used to compare. Add **er** to an adjective to compare two things. Add **est** to compare three or more things.

Joe's dog is small.
Tasha's dog is small**er**.
Anton's dog is small**est**.

Identify It
Read the sentences. Choose the correct adjective from the box. Write it on the line.

1. oldest older — Sami is the __oldest__ of all her sisters.
2. softer softest — Lola's pillow is __softer__ than mine.
3. louder loudest — My alarm clock is __louder__ than yours.
4. shorter shortest — Max has the __shortest__ hair of all.
5. slower slowest — Kiku's turtle is __slower__ than Alex's turtle.

Try It
Write two sentences. Compare two things in each sentence. Use these adjectives or one of your own: **harder, fastest, coldest, darker, youngest, longer**.

1. Answers will vary.
2.

143

Lesson 3.10 Comparative Adjectives

Complete It
Fill in the yellow spaces below with the correct adjective.

new	newer	newest
warm	warmer	**warmest**
hard	**harder**	hardest
neat	neater	**neatest**
smart	smarter	smartest
tall	**taller**	tallest

144

Lesson 3.11 Synonyms

Synonyms are words that mean the same or almost the same thing.
little, small   choose, pick   dad, father

Match It
Read each word. Find its synonym in the box. Write it in the matching mitten.

| jump | sleepy | glad |
| fast | shout | large |

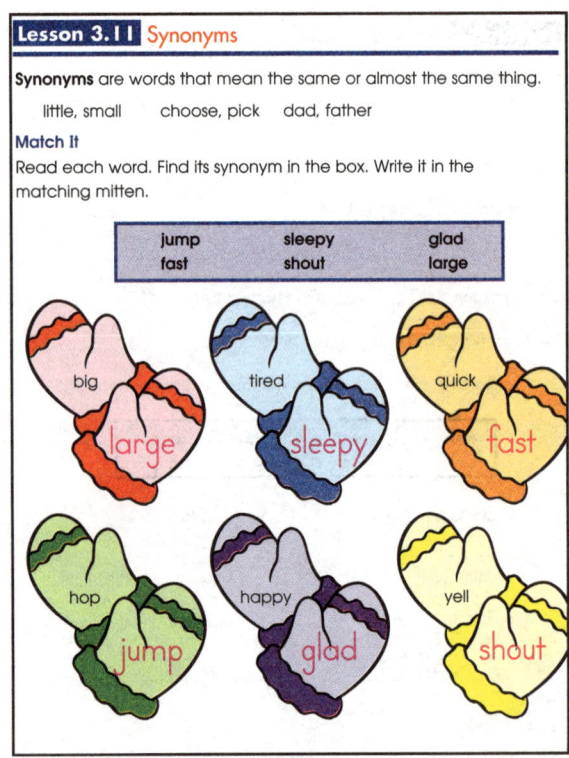

big — **large**
tired — **sleepy**
quick — **fast**
hop — **jump**
happy — **glad**
yell — **shout**

145

Spectrum Grade 1

Language Arts Grade 1 Answers

Lesson 3.11 Synonyms

Complete It
Read each sentence. Find a synonym in the box for the underlined word. Write the synonym on the line.

| toss | ship | small |
| begin | laughs | mother |

1. Please <u>throw</u> me that ball. — **toss**
2. My <u>mom</u> made waffles this morning. — **mother**
3. Don't <u>start</u> the movie without me. — **begin**
4. Luke has a <u>little</u> dog. — **small**
5. The <u>boat</u> is white and blue. — **ship**
6. Devi <u>giggles</u> at my jokes. — **laughs**

146

Lesson 3.12 Antonyms

Antonyms are words that are opposites.
hot, cold   black, white   old, young

Complete It
Fill in each blank with a word from the box.

| sad | front | go |
| night | down | full |

1. The opposite of **day** is **night**.
2. The opposite of **empty** is **full**.
3. The opposite of **happy** is **sad**.
4. The opposite of **up** is **down**.
5. The opposite of **stop** is **go**.
6. The opposite of **back** is **front**.

147

Lesson 3.12 Antonyms

Match It
Draw a line to match each word to its antonym.

right — wrong
first — last
new — old
win — lose
huge — tiny
in — out
quiet — loud

Try It
Draw a picture of two things that are opposites.

Pictures will vary

148

Lesson 3.13 Homophones

Homophones are words that sound the same. They have different spellings. They have different meanings, too.

to = toward — Throw it **to** me.
two = the number 2 — Nell has **two** cats.
too = also or very — Saki will come, **too**.
won = past tense of win — The Bears **won** the game!
one = the number 1 — **One** frog hopped away.
right = the opposite of left — Raise your **right** hand.
write = to put words on paper — Can you **write** your name?

Identify It
Underline the correct word to complete each sentence.

1. Jake bakes (won, <u>one</u>) cake.
2. Liam bakes (too, <u>two</u>) loaves of bread.
3. Reese can (<u>write</u>, right) down the recipes.
4. The flour is on the shelf on your (write, <u>right</u>).
5. Bella (<u>won</u>, one) first place in the bake-off!

149

Spectrum Grade 1

Language Arts Grade 1 Answers

Lesson 3.13 Homophones

Proof It
Make a line through each incorrect homophone. Write the correct word above it.

1. Carter will bring the muffins ~~two~~ **to** school.
2. Set up ~~too~~ **two** tables for the bake sale.
3. ~~Right~~ **Write** down the names of all the pies.
4. Only ~~won~~ **one** loaf of bread is left!

Try It
1. Write a sentence using the word **write**.
2. Write a se—

Answers will vary.

150

Lesson 3.14 Multiple-Meaning Words

Some words are spelled the same but have different meanings.

Pat caught a **cold** last week.   **cold** = an illness
It is **cold** outside.   **cold** = chilly; not warm

Match It
Read each sentence. Think about how the word in **bold** is used. Draw a line to the picture that shows it.

1. Ivan swung the **bat**.
2. The **bat** looked for some bugs to eat for dinner.
3. Maddy can tell time on her new **watch**.
4. **Watch** the birds in the tree.

151

Lesson 3.14 Multiple-Meaning Words

Try It
Read each pair of sentences. Look at the meaning of the first word in **bold**. Then, write the word's other meaning.

1. Did you hear the phone **ring**?
   ring: the sound a phone makes
   Kelly tried on Mom's wedding **ring**.
   ring: *something you wear on your finger*

2. **Park** the car across the street.
   park: to drive a car into a space
   There are new swings at the **park**.
   park: *a place to play outside*

3. We **saw** Ruby at the store.
   saw: watched or looked at
   Use the **saw** to cut the log.
   saw: *a sharp tool for cutting wood*

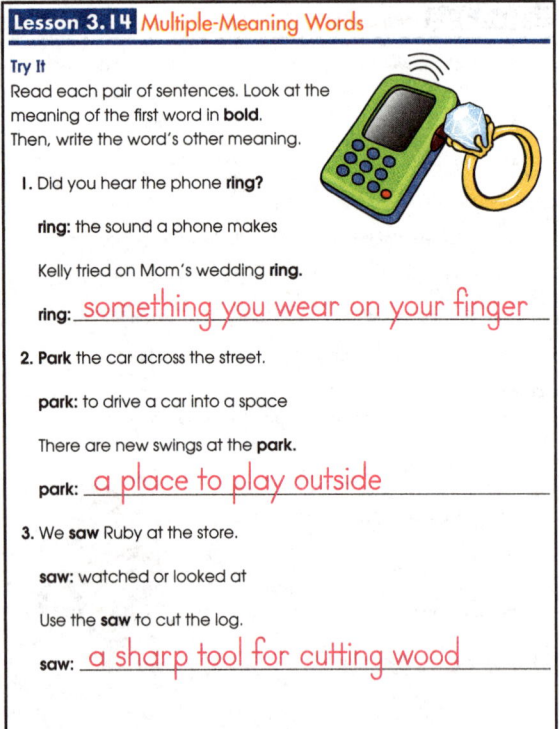

152

Spectrum Grade 1

Reading Grade 1 Answers

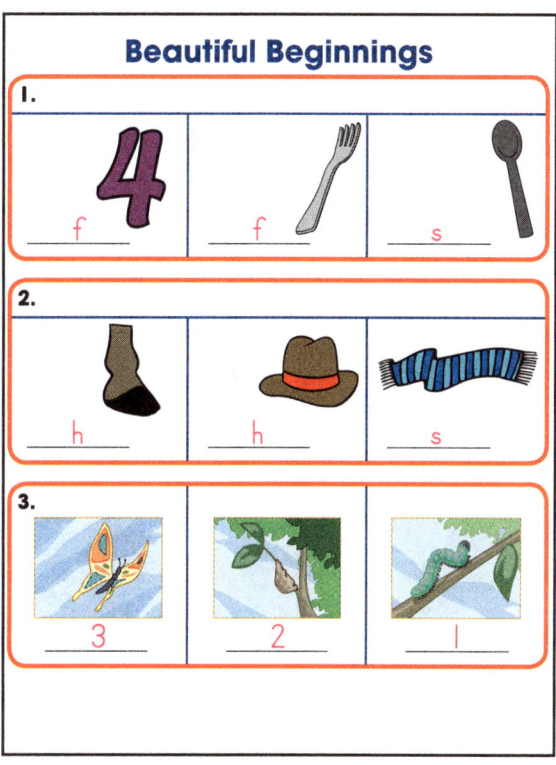

Reading Grade 1 Answers

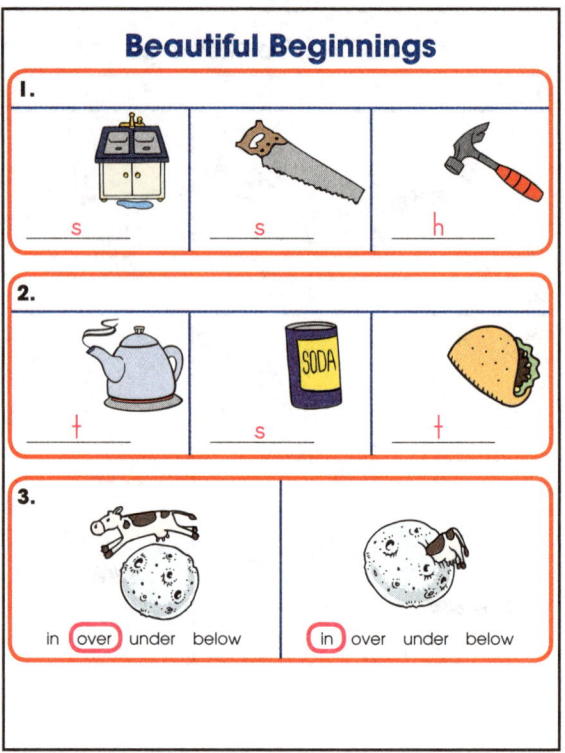

Reading Grade 1 Answers

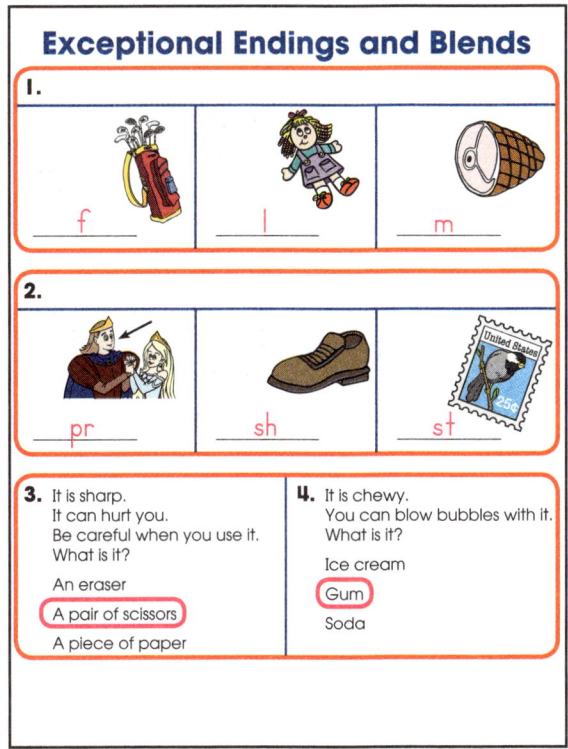

Reading Grade 1 Answers

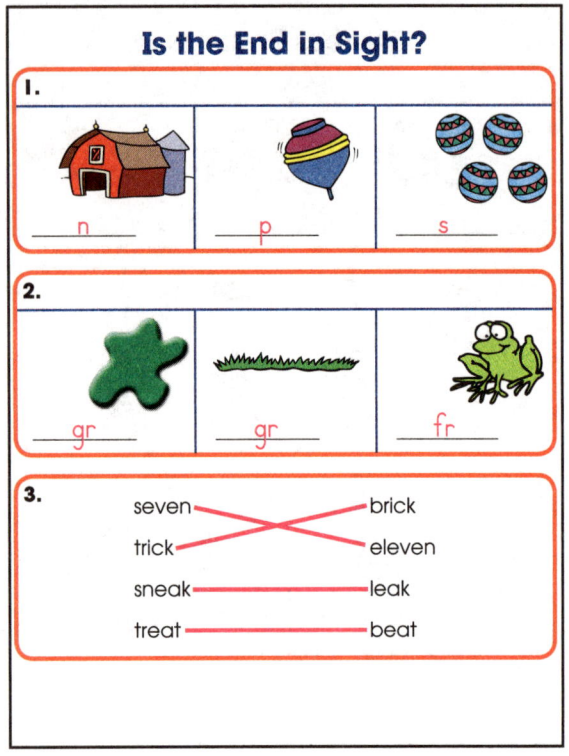

Spectrum Grade 1

Reading Grade 1 Answers

Dynamite Digraphs

1. wh ___ wh
2. i e i
3.
   - 3 The crowd cheers.
   - 1 The batter comes to the plate.
   - 2 The batter strikes out.

193

Beautiful Beginnings

1. i i i
2. tr
3. ch
4. sh
5. wh
6. th
7. dr

195

Go Short or Go Long: Aa

1. ate long
2. at short
3. ape long
4. act short
5. ant short
6. age long
7. rake long
8. ray long
9. able long
10. rat short
11. rack short
12. rate long
13. Andy short
14. Alex short
15. Abe long

197

Go Short or Go Long: Ee

1. pen short
2. pencil short
3. plea long
4. pea long
5. glee long
6. green long
7. tea long
8. ten short
9. teen long
10. hen short
11. fence short
12. bee long
13. be long
14. bend short
15. Ben short

199

Spectrum Grade 1
309

Reading Grade 1 Answers

Go Short or Go Long: Ii

1. pie long
2. pin short
3. pine long
4. pink short
5. pit short
6. tin short
7. time long
8. tiny long
9. tick short
10. Tim short
11. die long
12. dim short
13. diet long
14. dine long
15. dinner short

201

Go Short or Go Long: Oo

1. pot short
2. spot short
3. snow long
4. not short
5. oat long
6. on short
7. box short
8. mop short
9. rope long
10. Oliver short
11. show long
12. shop short
13. store short
14. stop short
15. slope long

203

Go Short or Go Long: Uu

1. under short
2. cube long
3. umbrella short
4. cut short
5. cute long
6. butter short
7. yummy short
8. mule long
9. club short
10. duck short
11. dune long
12. tuck short
13. tune long
14. run short
15. funny short

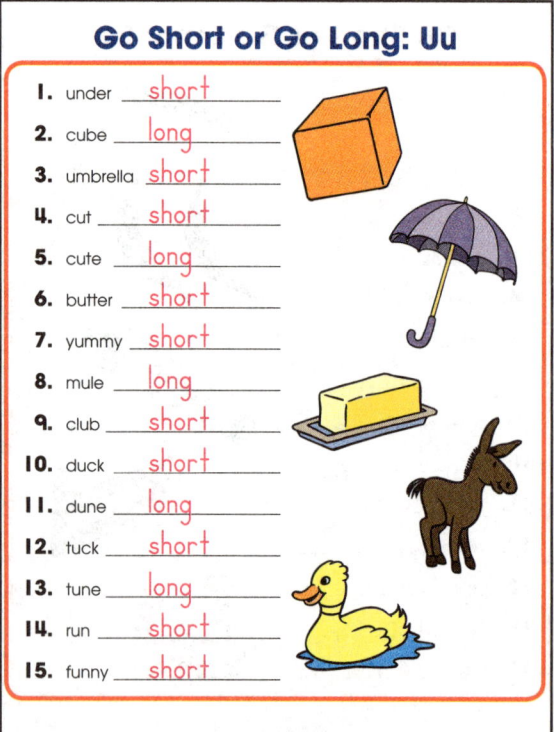

205

Big Time Rhyme

1. funny
2. honey
3. duck
4. stop
5. ton
6. snow
7. bear
8. spring
9. fall
10. tell
11. tear

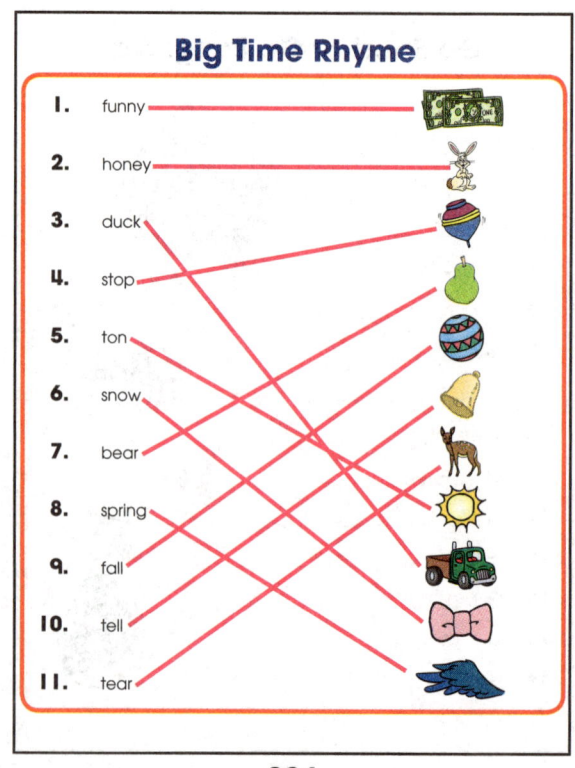

206

Spectrum Grade 1
310

Reading Grade 1 Answers

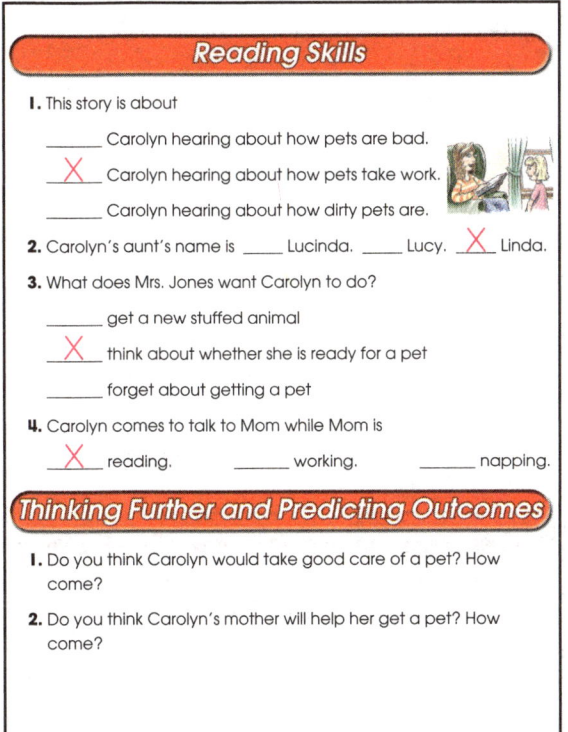

Reading Grade 1 Answers

Reading Skills

1. In this story,
   ____ Carolyn's dad tells her she can't have a pet.
   X Carolyn's dad talks about other types of pets.
   ____ Carolyn's dad says he will get her a dog.
2. Carolyn's dad mentions a possible pet. It is a
   X turtle.   ____ bunny.   ____ pony.
3. Who is the main character in the story?
   ____ Mrs. Jones
   ____ Mr. Jones
   X Carolyn
4. Carolyn's mom and dad ____ about pets being a lot of work.
   X agree   ____ do not agree

Thinking Further and Predicting Outcomes

1. Do you think Carolyn would enjoy a pet turtle?
2. Do you think Carolyn's dad knows why she wants a pet? Why or why not?

215

Reading Skills

1. In this story,
   X Carolyn explains how she would take care of her new pet.
   ____ Carolyn says she is sad.
   ____ Carolyn talks about her friends at school.
2. The pet will be named ____ Prince. **X** Promise. ____ Misty.
3. This story takes place
   X in the morning.   ____ at lunchtime.   ____ before bed.
4. When will Carolyn's parents tell her their answer?
   X tomorrow   ____ Monday   ____ after lunch
5. Who is telling the story?
   ____ Carolyn   **X** the author   ____ Carolyn's mom

Thinking Further and Predicting Outcomes

1. Do you think Carolyn has explained herself well? How do you know?
2. Do you think Carolyn's parents like her plan? Why or why not?

217

Reading Skills

1. This story is about
   X Carolyn waking up early to find out if she will get a pet.
   ____ Carolyn waking up early to go to school.
   ____ Carolyn sleeping because she is so tired.
2. Carolyn's last name is **X** Jones.   ____ Promise.   ____ Linda.
3. Which of these is NOT something Carolyn will do for her pet?
   ____ brush its fur
   ____ love it
   X clip its nails
4. Look at the picture on page 218. Carolyn looks
   X excited.   ____ sneaky.   ____ grumpy.

Thinking Further and Predicting Outcomes

1. What will the decision be?
2. Why do people love pets?
3. How do you think Carolyn feels as she comes running down the stairs?

219

Reading Skills

1. This story is about
   X Carolyn finding out that she will get a pet.
   ____ Carolyn finding out that she will not get a pet.
   ____ Carolyn finding out she's late for school.
2. Carolyn hugged her ____ mother.   ____ father.   **X** parents.
3. Carolyn's dad has a big smile on his face when he has something _____ to say.
   ____ strange   **X** good   ____ bad
4. What is the setting for this story?
   X the kitchen
   ____ the den
   ____ Carolyn's bedroom

Thinking Further and Predicting Outcomes

1. Where will the Jones family get their pet?
2. Do you think Carolyn's parents made the right decision? How come?

221

Spectrum Grade 1

Reading Grade 1 Answers

Reading Skills

223

1. This story is about
   - **X** Carolyn telling her friends about getting a pet.
   - ____ Carolyn telling her friends about her school project.
   - ____ Carolyn's visit to the pound.
2. What was the name of Carolyn's friend who asked about her new pet? His name is
   - **X** Freddy.   ____ Eddie.   ____ Betty.
3. Carolyn tells Freddy that she would like to get a puppy or
   - ____ an alligator.
   - **X** a kitten.
   - ____ a goldfish.
4. Where will the Jones family go to get a pet?
   - **X** the pound   ____ the pet store   ____ a farm

Thinking Further and Predicting Outcomes

1. Do you think Carolyn will show her pet to her classmates? Why or why not?

Reading Skills

225

1. This story is about
   - **X** Carolyn learning about the pound.
   - ____ Carolyn wanting to go to the pet store.
   - ____ Carolyn changing her mind about getting a pet.
2. Mrs. Jones and Carolyn will go to the
   - **X** pound.   ____ pet store.   ____ zoo.
3. In the picture above, what is Carolyn thinking about?
   - ____ a stuffed dog   ____ a teddy bear   **X** a real dog
4. Which kind of animal will Carolyn and her mom NOT see at the pound?
   - ____ cats   ____ rabbits   **X** chickens

Thinking Further and Predicting Outcomes

1. Do you think it's a good idea to go to the pound for a pet? Why or why not?
2. What will Carolyn do when she chooses her pet?

Reading Skills

227

1. This story is about
   - **X** Carolyn seeing all sorts of animals at the pound.
   - ____ Carolyn feeling scared.
   - ____ Carolyn playing with a lizard.
2. Carolyn plays with a kitten that is
   - ____ eating.   **X** sleeping.   ____ drinking.
3. How did the fat cat's tongue feel on Carolyn's hand?
   - **X** scratchy   ____ soft   ____ slimy
4. There was only one kind of animal at the pound.
   - ____ true
   - **X** false

Thinking Further and Predicting Outcomes

1. Will Carolyn choose a pet after all? How do you know?
2. Will Carolyn get more than one pet? How do you know?
3. What kinds of words are used to describe the dogs?
   fat, skinny, furry

Reading Skills

229

1. This story is about
   - **X** Carolyn realizing that taking care of only one pet is still a good thing.
   - ____ Carolyn realizing that she should take five pets.
   - ____ Carolyn leaving the pound with no pets.
2. The pets are living in **X** cages.   ____ houses.   ____ boxes.
3. The pound needs more
   - ____ cats.   ____ dogs.   **X** workers.
4. Carolyn wishes that all the animals had someone to ____ them.
   - ____ wash   **X** love   ____ name

Thinking Further and Predicting Outcomes

1. Do you think Carolyn will feel better about taking only one pet? How come?
2. Do you think Carolyn is a caring person? Why or why not?
3. The next time Carolyn gets a pet, do you think she will go to the pound again? Why or why not?

Spectrum Grade 1

Reading Grade 1 Answers

Reading Skills

1. This story is about
   - **X** Carolyn choosing a kitten.
   - _____ Carolyn choosing a puppy.
   - _____ Carolyn choosing two puppies.
2. What color is the kitten? **X** white _____ black _____ brown
3. Which sentence is true?
   - _____ Mom had to choose for Carolyn.
   - **X** Carolyn chose the sleeping kitten.
   - _____ Carolyn decided to get a kitten and a puppy.
4. Carolyn thinks the kitten looks like
   - **X** a baby cloud. _____ a snowball. _____ a cotton ball.

Thinking Further and Predicting Outcomes

1. Do you think Carolyn will always take good care of her kitten? How come?
2. Do you think Carolyn will be happy with her new pet? Why or why not?

231

Reading Skills

1. In this story,
   - **X** Carolyn realizes she cannot have her kitten until tomorrow.
   - _____ Carolyn learns that the kitten belongs to someone.
   - _____ Carolyn learns that the kitten is 3 years old.
2. The kitten is a **X** boy. _____ girl.
3. Before the kitten can come home with Carolyn, it needs to have its _____.
   - _____ food   **X** shots   _____ training
4. Mrs. Jones thinks that the kitten is
   - _____ too little. _____ too wild. **X** beautiful.

Thinking Further and Predicting Outcomes

1. Do you think Carolyn will be upset that she can't have the kitten right away? How come?
2. Do you think Carolyn will be nervous for the kitten because he needs shots? How come?

233

Reading Skills

1. This story is about
   - **X** Carolyn getting a gift from her dad.
   - _____ Carolyn learning to study.
   - _____ Carolyn playing with Promise.
2. The new kitten is like a
   - **X** cotton ball. _____ paper. _____ snow.
3. Carolyn's dad asks if they should call the kitten Cloudy or
   - _____ Buttons. _____ Snowy. **X** Mr. Cotton.
4. What does Mr. Jones buy as a gift for Promise Jones?
   - **X** a cat bed _____ a scratching post _____ litter

Thinking Further and Predicting Outcomes

1. Do you think Carolyn makes the right decision about keeping Promise's name the same? Why?
2. Do you like soft things? Why?
3. If you got a kitten, what would you name it?

235

Reading Skills

1. This story is about
   - **X** Carolyn promising to care for her cat.
   - _____ Carolyn eating dinner with her cat.
   - _____ Carolyn having a party with her parents.
2. Carolyn plays with her new pet in the
   - _____ bedroom. **X** family room. _____ kitchen.
3. How do you think Promise Jones felt?
   - **X** shy _____ sad _____ lazy
4. What is Carolyn's promise to her new kitten?
   - _____ She will play with him every day.
   - _____ She will not get any more pets.
   - **X** He has found a home.

Thinking Further and Predicting Outcomes

1. Do you think Carolyn will ever want another pet? Why?
2. Would you want somebody like Carolyn as your friend? Why or why not?

237

Spectrum Grade 1

Reading Grade 1 Answers

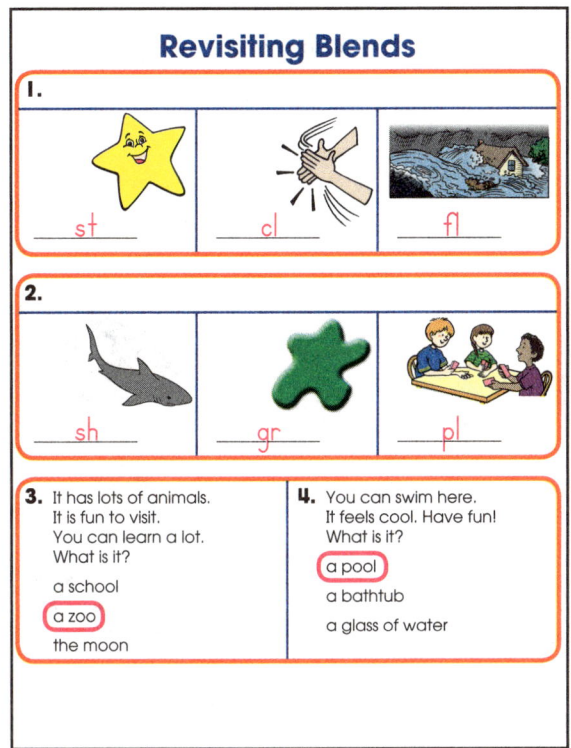

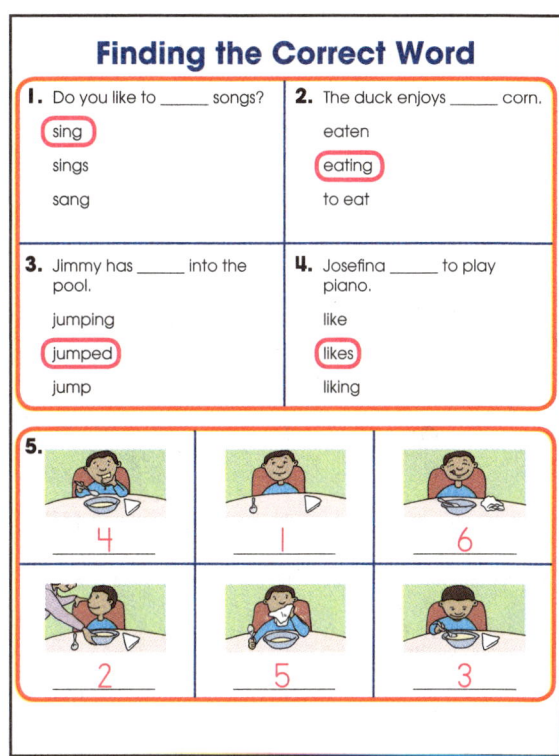

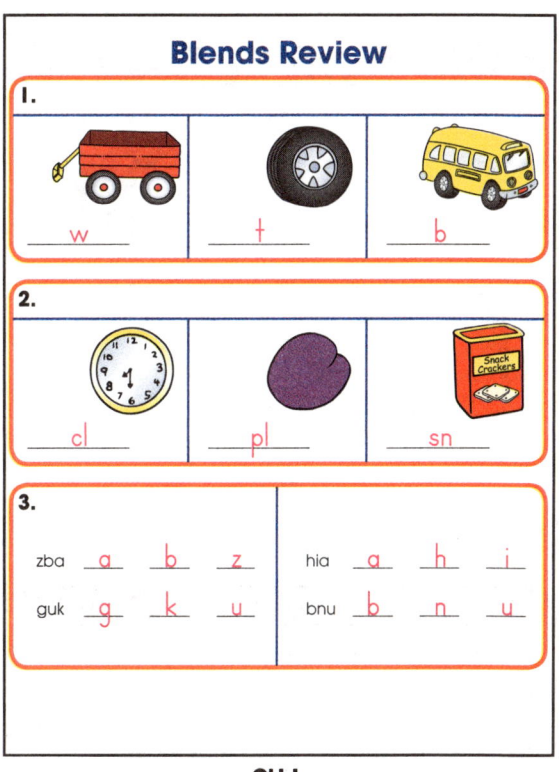

Reading Grade 1 Answers

242

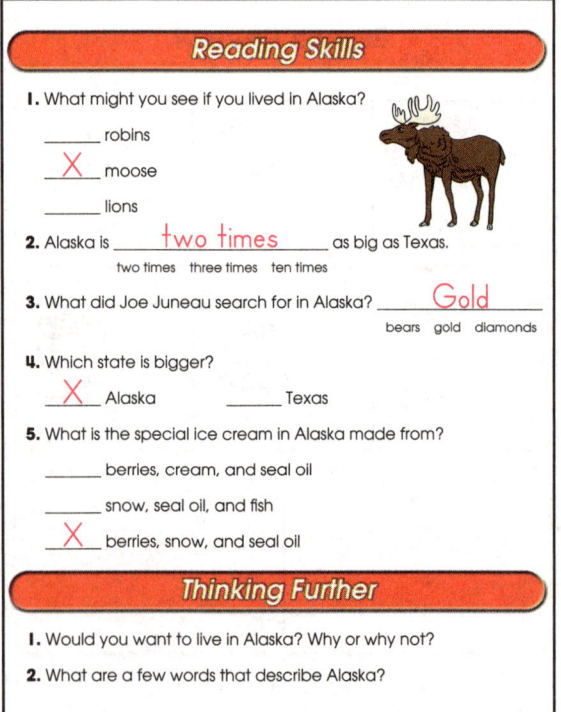

245

243

Classify Me

1. (three) (six) (five) food
2. (orange) (lemon) (lime) ham
3. (penny) (dime) (nickel) dollar
4. (mouse) (rat) bug (lion)
5. (truck) (car) boat (bus)
6. (June) (July) (August) flag
7. (green) (yellow) (brown) tired
8. (stone) (rock) (brick) rug
9. (mom) (dad) dog (sister)
10. (funny) (smile) (laugh) mad

247

Reading Skills

1. What might you see if you lived in New Mexico?
   - X bunches of chili peppers
   - ___ bunches of bananas
   - ___ bunches of green peppers
2. Santa Fe was founded in X 1610. ___ 1615. ___ 1910.
3. Adobe houses are made from _____ bricks.
   - X clay   ___ rock   ___ concrete
4. Why does Santa Fe have a star next to it on the map of New Mexico?
   - ___ The author lives there.
   - ___ It is the biggest city.
   - X It is the capital.

Thinking Further

1. Would you want to live in New Mexico? Why or why not?
2. What are a few words that describe New Mexico?
3. Were you surprised to find out that it snows in New Mexico? Why or why not?

Spectrum Grade 1
316

Reading Grade 1 Answers

Reading Skills (249)

1. What might you see if you visited Oregon?
   - **X** the deepest lake
   - ____ the widest lake
   - ____ the coldest lake

2. Some people went to Oregon because it had __rich__ soil.
   rich   poor   dirty

A **table of contents** tells you where to find things in a book. Use this table of contents to answer the questions.

Table of Contents
Map of Oregon 3
The Oregon Trail 5
Oregon's Natural Beauty 17
Famous People of Oregon 25
Oregon Today 33

3. If you want to find out about Oregon's national parks, turn to page (5, **17**).

4. If you want to find out where the city of Portland, Oregon is, turn to page (**3**, 25).

Thinking Further

1. Do you think there are farmers in Oregon? How do you know?
2. What are a few words that describe Oregon?

Reading Skills (251)

1. What island could you see in Rhode Island?
   - **X** Block Island
   - ____ Kidd Island
   - ____ Watch Island

2. Rhode Island is the __smallest__ state.
   smallest   largest   prettiest

3. Rhode Island has a nickname. It is
   - **X** "Little Rhody."
   - ____ "Bay State."
   - ____ "Pirate State."

4. If you wanted to go to Block Island, you could take a
   - **X** ferry.   ____ train.   ____ bus.

Thinking Further

1. Would you want to travel to Block Island? Why or why not?
2. Give Rhode Island another nickname.
3. Do you think that Captain Kidd's gold is still buried on Block Island? Why or why not?

Reading Skills (253)

1. What might you see if you live in Vermont?
   - **X** green mountains
   - ____ green rivers
   - ____ blue mountains

2. You can climb
   - **X** Bread Loaf Mountain.
   - ____ Meatloaf Mountain.
   - ____ Butter Mountain.

3. Maple tree sap is turned into syrup. This happens in a
   - ____ milk house.   **X** sugarhouse.   ____ sap house.

4. What does Vermont's name mean?
   - ____ Tall Mountains
   - ____ Maple Mountains
   - **X** Green Mountains

5. Vermont's name comes from two _____ words.
   - ____ Spanish   ____ German   **X** French

Thinking Further

1. Would you want to live in Vermont? Why or why not?
2. What kind of tree is in the picture on page 252? How do you know? __maple; It is being tapped for syrup.__

Reading Skills (255)

1. Robert Frost was a famous
   - ____ songwriter.
   - **X** poet.
   - ____ singer.

2. Many of his poems are about
   - ____ roses.   ____ buildings.   **X** nature.

3. What do you think Robert Frost would rather write a poem about?
   - ____ bikes   **X** trees   ____ trucks

4. Which of these statements is NOT true?
   - ____ Robert Frost lived in a town called Derry.
   - ____ Robert Frost wrote poems about fall leaves.
   - **X** No one knows where Robert got his ideas.

Thinking Further

1. Would you want to live in New Hampshire? Why or why not?
2. What would you like to write a poem about?

Spectrum Grade 1

Reading Grade 1 Answers

Reading Skills

1. Montana is called
   ___ "Big Time."
   _X_ "Big Sky Country."
   ___ "Big Cow."
2. Grasshopper Glacier has _____ of frozen grasshoppers.
   ___ a couple   ___ hundreds   _X_ millions
3. Why are the Rocky Mountain goats hard to see?
   ___ There are only a few of them.
   ___ They blend in with the mountain.
   _X_ They live high up on the rocks.
4. In Montana, the sky seems to meet the
   _X_ land.   ___ sea.   ___ lake.

Thinking Further

1. Would you want to live in Montana? Why or why not?
2. Which would you want to see more, a grasshopper, glacier, or a Rocky Mountain goat? Explain why.

257

Reading Skills

1. Nevada is the _____ state in the United States.
   ___ rainiest
   _X_ driest
   ___ hottest
2. Huge piles of cement were used to make Hoover Dam
   _X_ strong.   ___ gray.   ___ cold.
3. Who was Hoover Dam named after?
   ___ the person who built it
   _X_ a president
   ___ the governor of Nevada
4. The water in Lake Tahoe is
   _X_ clear.   ___ cloudy.   ___ shallow.

Thinking Further

1. Would you want to live in Nevada? Why or why not?
2. Would you want to help build a giant water dam? Why or why not?

259

Reading Skills

1. Over _____ islands make up Hawaii.
   _X_ one hundred
   ___ two hundred
   ___ three hundred
2. The word *aloha* means
   ___ like.   ___ pretty.   _X_ love.
3. Volcanoes make Hawaii's
   _X_ islands.   ___ weather.   ___ oceans.
4. Saying *aloha* is a way to _____ people.
   ___ confuse
   _X_ welcome
   ___ call

Thinking Further

1. Would you want to live in Hawaii? Why or why not?
2. Would you want to tour a volcano?
3. What is unusual about some of the plants and animals in Hawaii?
   They are not found anywhere else.

261

Reading Skills

1. What might you see in Maryland?
   _X_ bays
   ___ a rain forest
   ___ the tallest mountain
2. Maryland has things to do for
   _X_ everybody.   ___ a few people.
3. Which of these is Maryland's nickname?
   ___ "little America"   ___ "the Bay State"
   _X_ "mini America"
4. Francis Scott Key was on a _____ in a harbor when he wrote America's anthem.
   ___ plane   _X_ boat   ___ beach

Thinking Further

1. Would you like to live in Maryland? Why or why not?
2. What would you nickname Maryland?
3. How do you think Maryland got its nickname?
   Possible answer: It has mountains, valleys, and beaches, just like America does.

263

Spectrum Grade 1

Reading Grade 1 Answers

Page 264

Reading Skills

1. What might you see in California?
   - **X** movie making
   - ___ cornfields
   - ___ kangaroos

2. Why do so many people visit California?
   - **X** There are many pretty places to visit.
   - ___ There are lots of cars.
   - ___ There are lots of people.

3. Based on the article, you know that California is near
   - **X** the ocean.   ___ Florida.   ___ a big lake.

4. **California is the largest state.** Is this true or false?
   - ___ true   **X** false

Thinking Further

1. Would you like to live in California? Why or why not?
2. What would you nickname California?
3. Look at the picture near the top of this page. What does it help you understand about California?
   How big redwood trees are.

Page 267

Reading Skills

1. Winters in Minnesota can be so cold that wet hair turns to
   - ___ snow.
   - **X** ice.
   - ___ dark.

2. Where might you go swimming in Minnesota?
   - **X** lakes   ___ parks   ___ oceans

3. The cities of Minneapolis and St. Paul are known as the
   - ___ "Double Cities."   **X** "Twin Cities."
   - ___ "Chilly Cities."

4. Fishing and boating are fun to do in Minnesota during the
   - ___ winter.   **X** summer.

Thinking Further

1. Would you want to visit Minnesota? Why or why not?
2. What are two words that describe Minnesota?
3. If you lived in Minnesota, would you like summer or winter better? Why?

Page 269

Reading Skills

1. The city of Denver is _____ in the sky.
   - ___ low
   - **X** high
   - ___ blue

2. Some people come to this state to
   - **X** ski.   ___ surf.   ___ see fish.

3. What is the capital of Colorado?
   - ___ Rocky Mountain
   - ___ Mile City
   - **X** Denver

Thinking Further

1. Would you like to ski, bike, or raft in Colorado? Why?
2. What are two words to describe Colorado?
3. What does the red star by Denver on the map mean?
   It means that Denver is the capital of Colorado.

Page 270

Words to Know

1. **duck**, dog, did
2. for, **fish**, from
3. **grass**, green, go
4. **bowl**, bee, big
5. call, can't, **cold**
6. **water**, wet, won't
7. **pond**, put, play
8. **foot**, farm, for
9. can, class, **corn**
10. hop, **hat**, him
11. **road**, run, red
12. **sun**, son, sit
13. pull, push, **pail**
14. **soft**, set, says
15. sleep, slip, **sled**

Spectrum Grade 1
319

Reading Grade 1 Answers

271

272

273

274

275